Introduction to Chinese Culture

Chung Mou Si
Yun Cheng Si

图书在版编目（CIP）数据

中华文化精粹：英／Chung Mou Si，Yun Cheng Si 编著．—北京：北京大学出版社，2011.3

ISBN 978-7-301-18528-5

Ⅰ．中… Ⅱ．①S… ②S… Ⅲ．传统文化－中国－普及读物－英 Ⅳ．G12-49

中国版本图书馆 CIP 数据核字 (2011) 第 017212 号

书　　　名：中华文化精粹
　　　　　　Introduction to Chinese Culture
著作责任者：Chung Mou Si　Yun Cheng Si 编著
责 任 编 辑：邓晓霞　dxxvip@yahoo.com.cn
标 准 书 号：ISBN 978-7-301-18528-5 / G · 3081
出 版 社：北京大学出版社
地　　　址：北京市海淀区成府路 205 号 100871
网　　　址：http://www.pup.cn
电　　　话：邮购部 62752015　发行部 62750672
　　　　　　编辑部 62754144　出版部 62754962
电 子 信 箱：zpup@pup.pku.edu.cn
印 刷 者：北京大学印刷厂
经 销 者：新华书店
　　　　　　650 毫米 ×980 毫米　16 开本　13.25 印张　278 千字
　　　　　　2011 年 3 月第 1 版　　2011 年 3 月第 1 次印刷
定　　　价：56.00 元

Foreword

It is not uncommon today for visitors to China to be awestruck by the hyper-modern shape of the nation's major cities. The steel and glass skyscrapers reflect both the buzz of life on the streets below and the cranes on the skyline constructing the next architectural wonder alongside. The impact of the country's double digit growth rates is evident everywhere in China's major urban centres.

Confronted with such dramatic twenty-first century hyper-modernity it is easy to forget the narratives that formed China's lengthy history and underpin her current success. While iconic structures such as The Great Wall and the Forbidden City stand as reminders of the power of dynasties past, the cultural logic that made such wonders of cultural heritage meaningful is not so evident. China's awe-inspiring past is connected directly to its equally awe-inspiring present by a common set of core stories that everyone raised in China cannot help but know. *Introduction to Chinese Culture* provides readers with precisely these core narratives that have sustained Chinese culture for centuries.

Despite all the shifts in economic, military, political and developmental spheres, there is a popularly embraced common knowledge about Chinese culture that the Chinese people feel is fundamentally theirs at the core. Professor CM Si and his team have gathered the most important of these together to create an enlightening and accessible volume. It introduces readers to the key aspects of Chinese culture and brings the stories behind the key locations and personages together.

They have compiled this illustrated volume of 56 succinct essays grouped within 8 chapters, to cover the core myths, festivals, historical sights, food and sports, arts and crafts, language and literature, philosophy and international connections. These iconic stories, localities and cultural practices stretch back thousands of years and have emerged from amidst myriad other possible competitors as the foundational cultural grammar of twenty-first century China. Professor Si has drawn on his extensive experience in teaching and deep knowledge of Chinese culture to select the core components from amidst China's vast cultural heritage.

These essays not only tell readers about 'traditions' but they also tell us how these traditions have changed over time and transformed into contemporary practices and beliefs. We learn about how festivals evolve over time to cope with new social forces while still maintaining their integrity as time-honored 'traditions'. Professor Si explains how early Chinese scientific concepts that explained the nature of the world interacted with other types of science from around the world. We learn about the way that long-standing Chinese concepts of 'the calculation of time' in the annual cycle altered in relation to contact with Europe — but also how the Chinese calendar remains as a core marker for foundational cultural events such as Spring Festival, Yuanxiao and Qingming.

Taken as a whole, the chapters create a lively picture of how complex interpersonal relations experienced by ordinary people throughout the centuries — such as love and romance; birth and death; friendship and loyalty — have been negotiated through storytelling. We also learn about the complex connection between individuals and their leaders through the chapters on the imperial dynasties through to the contemporary government with its 56 national minorities.

In sum, this book will be invaluable to all students of Chinese culture but also to the educated observer of world cultures and travelers to China. In understanding the foundational principles underlying Chinese culture, readers will be able to make far better sense of the uniqueness of the twenty-first century China that they see before them. Moreover, readers will recognize the features that Professor Si has narrated in the dynamics of the myriad Chinese communities in Asia, Africa, the Americas and Europe.

Congratulations to Professor Si and to Peking University Press for their foresight in producing such an accessible and lively introduction to the core of Chinese culture. China's importance to the world is more evident today than it has been for decades and this book will go a long way to ensuring enhanced knowledge of the culture that underpins the twenty-first century superpower.

Professor Louise Edwards (FAHA, FASSA)
The University of Hong Kong
Modern China Program

Contents

Contents

Chapter 4 Food and Sports

Chapter 5 Arts and Crafts

Chapter 6 Language and Literature

Contents

Chapter 7 Thought and Enlightenment

Chapter 8 China and the World

Appendix

Chapter 1

Myths and Legends

1 How the World Was Created

Filling the Hole in the Sky

Where do our ancestors come from? How was nature formed? These questions were raised centuries ago. Different religions and all sorts of myths from various cultures attempted to provide explanations and answers to these questions, so as to satisfy human curiosity.

In the West, many people believe that God created the world, as well as every creature and things. However in China, people believe that it was a man called Pangu who created the world, and then transformed himself into different creatures and things. Nowadays temples can be found in numerous cities in China where he is worshipped.

Now you may ask, what

was the story? A long time ago, the Chinese believed that the universe was simply a mixture of gas, with absolutely nothing in it. There was a person whose name was Pangu. He was sad to see the world in such a state and felt that he should do something about it. He grabbed a hammer in one hand and an axe in the other, and then by using some mysterious power, he managed to separate the gas, forming the sky and the land.

Unfortunately, Pangu overworked himself and became really weak. Suddenly, something amazing happened. His breath became wind and clouds, his voice became thunder; his left eye transformed into the sun while his right eye transformed into the moon; his limbs became huge mountains, his blood became rivers, his blood vessels became land patterns, his muscles became fields and land; his hair turned into stars, his body hair turned into grass and trees, his teeth and bones turned into various minerals, his bone marrow turned into precious stones and gems, his sweat turned into rain and dew, and the little worms all over his body turned into millions of people.

Westerners believe that God created human and Gods are superior to us. However this is not the case for the Chinese. The Chinese think that they all have Pangu's power in their bodies. They regard themselves as the brightest among all living creatures, who have the power to overcome challenges and unfortunate circumstances. It is this belief in their power that has driven them forward for so many years. Many apparatus were invented to observe, calculate and read climate changes from nature, so as to avoid catastrophes.

You might be thinking that after the world was created, everything would settle down and start growing. Not so. It happened that one day, the God of Water and the God of Fire had a huge fight ending in a victory for the God of Fire. The God of

Water, being the loser, was extremely frustrated and ashamed of himself. He was so angry that he bumped against the Buzhou Mountain which served to support the sky and separate it from the land. The result of this impetuous act was that, half the sky crumbled, opening up an enormous gaping hole. Through this hole, water from the river up in the sky ran down and flooded the land below. The whole world was in a complete mess.

The creator-goddess, Nüwa, felt upset at the sight of such a disaster, and she decided to fix it. From the river, she collected 36,501 multi-coloured stones, burning them with a fierce fire for seven whole days, turning them into lava. Then she took a big spoon, and began splashing spoonfuls of lava against the hole in the sky. Soon, the lava condensed and the hole was filled. After taking care of the sky, Nüwa then turned her attention to the submerged land. She burned huge amounts of weeds into ashes, which she used to fill up the flooded areas, and eventually the land reappeared. Everything went back to normal. From then on, the colours in the sky were explained by Nüwa's use of those multi-coloured stones.

To prevent such disasters from happening again, Nüwa started to look for suitable materials to use as pillars to hold up the sky. A sea turtle came to her and offered to help. She thought that was perfect, so she agreed to let the four legs of the turtle become the pillars of the sky. However, the world had become slightly different after the fight. The leg of the turtle that was holding up the north-western side of the sky was shorter than the others, which is why the sun, the moon and the stars all travel towards that direction. On the other hand, when the land crumbled, the south-eastern side crumbled most significantly. As a result, rivers in China all flow to the south-east.

You may recall that Nüwa collected 36,501 pieces of multi-coloured stones. After she finished her repair work, she realised that a piece of stone was left unused. She decided to keep the stone for herself, but she accidentally dropped the stone as she travelled back to heaven. The final destination of this stone has become a mystery for people to ponder. Some say, it became the Yellow Mountain (also known as Huang Shan). Some say, it became the Pearl of the Orient — Hong Kong.

2 The Dog from the Sky

With all our current advanced technology, various scientific discoveries have been made and many mysterious occurrences can now be explained using scientific evidence. Nowadays, we all know how the solar and lunar eclipses occur. However, back in the old days, there was no way people could understand this. When a total or a near-total solar eclipse happens, the sky darkens in the daytime. Centuries ago, people were frightened by this darkening of the sky. In order to ease people's worries and ease their fears, the Chinese came up with a story that explained the occurrence of eclipses.

The ancient Chinese believed that a lunar eclipse was the result of a dog from the sky eating the moon. But why would the dog eat the moon? There was a couple from the tribe of Lisu; the husband was called Gelishi, the wife was called Dumawu, and together they raised a dog. Every night, the couple spent time together dancing and enjoying themselves under the moonlight. Gradually, Gelishi developed a huge interest in the moon, and he started to wonder what exactly the moon was. Even after observing the moon for a long time and thinking hard, he still could not get a satisfactory answer. So he decided to use bamboo as a ladder to the sky, so that he could take a closer look at the moon and find out exactly what it was.

Before starting his journey, Gelishi said to his wife, "Dumawu, after I'm gone, please remember, water the bamboo to keep it alive and maintain its growth. If the bamboo withers and dies, I will fall from the sky." With tears in her eyes, hoping that he would stay, she begged him, "I'm about to give birth to our baby, please don't go." He comforted her, "Don't worry, I will be back very soon!"

Gelishi took the dog with him and they started climbing up the ladder. On and on they went, and there were no signs of their return. Dumawu kept watering the bamboo, until she was about to give birth to her baby. At that time, she was in extreme pain and was so weak that she could not even leave her bed. Consequently, the bamboo withered. At this very moment, Gelishi and the dog were just about to reach the moon, so the dog made a final leap and landed on the moon, while he stretched out his arms to grab onto the moon. All of a sudden, there was a very loud noise, the ladder had snapped into pieces, and he fell from the sky.

Since the ladder was gone, the dog could never return to earth. There was no food on the moon, so when the dog was hungry, it

A Lunar Eclipse

could only eat the moon. Whenever there is a lunar eclipse ancient Chinese believed it was the dog eating the moon. The Lisu people feared that the dog would one day eat the whole moon, so they prepared pigs and lambs as sacrifices when they noticed that part of the moon was disappearing, in the hope that the dog would not eat the whole moon. A similar story evolved for solar eclipses. The ancient Chinese would play musical instruments or make loud noises to frighten the dog from "eating the sun", all the while praying to their Gods for protection.

3 | Shooting down the Sun

With all our numerous scientific discoveries and technological developments over the past couple of centuries, people are now starting to pay attention to the side effects of such advances, such as, global warming. It has gradually become a common topic for scientific, governmental and even business conferences, while pressure groups are producing videos to promote the idea of preventing global warming. Latest reports suggest that if the current rate of temperature rise is not halted or at least slowed down, 37% of the species on earth will disappear forever in 40 years' time, in other words, over a million kinds of creatures and plants face the prospect of extinction. This would be the biggest disaster in terms of extinction of species since the disappearance of dinosaurs.

You would think that this would be the first time humans have faced such a situation. However, dinosaurs lived on the earth much earlier than people and Chinese beliefs also suggest otherwise. Thousands of years ago, there were 10 suns in the sky. They were all sons of the Heavenly God. They had to take turns to be on duty in the sky to provide light and heat to the people on earth. Days passed by, and they started to feel bored. One day, they thought, why not go on duty together? And they did just that. The presence of the 10 suns together drained rivers and caused the wilting of plants due to excessive evaporation. People felt like they were trapped in an extremely hot furnace.

The Heavenly God saw this, and decided to send Hou Yi to persuade his 10 sons to stop doing this. However, the 10 suns were having so much fun that they simply ignored him. This greatly enraged him. Hou took the Bow of Heaven, loaded a magical arrow, and shot. The first shot took down one of the suns, and then 8 shots later, 9 suns had been taken down. The leftover sun was shivering with fright, hiding behind layers of thick cloud. Hou was just about to take the tenth shot when people reminded him that if all the suns were gone, the world would be in total darkness. He realised that they were right, so he stopped at once and left. Everything then started to go back to normal.

Shooting down the sun

The sun has always been a symbol of hope. Since ancient times, people of all races have realised that the sun is essential to our lives. The sun provides us with light and heat that are the basic components for the growth of all plants and creatures on earth. Because of its mysterious and magical power, people have always respected the sun greatly, some even to the extent of fearing it. As well as respecting the sun, people are also curious about it, and as a result, there is always a deity representing the sun in most ancient cultures. For example, in China there are these 10 sons of the Heavenly God representing the 10 suns; in Greece, there is Helius who is the God of the Sun; and in Egypt there is Ra.

Together with the previous two stories, we can see that the Chinese believed that the ancient gods made huge efforts to provide us with a better environment to live in. Unfortunately, people have now created problems like global warming, acid rain, all sorts of pollution, deforestation, soil erosion and the extinction of species, just to name a few. Since we have realised that we are destroying the earth, it is still not too late to try to reduce the damage, and try to protect and preserve the environment so that the earth will become a better place to live in. We can count on the Chinese to do their part, by continuing the good deeds of their ancient gods in saving the earth for their offspring.

4 The Old Man under the Moon

There is a very famous Chinese saying which goes like this: "The marriage of two people from thousands of miles away is brought together by a string." What people may not know is that, there is an interesting story behind this saying. It was said that during the Tang Dynasty (618 – 907), there was a man named Wei Gu. One night, Wei came across an old man leaning against a cloth sack, flipping through a book under the light of the moon. His curiosity aroused, Wei asked the old man what he was reading, and the old man told him, "It is *The Book of Marriage*. All marriages in this world are recorded in it." He then asked what was inside the sack. The old man told him that it was a red string which was used to fix marriages. So, whenever a male and a female were tied together by this red string, they would get married at some point in the future. Upon hearing such answers, he just shook his head in disbelief.

Wei then asked the old man who would be his future wife. At that time, a blind woman was passing by, holding a little girl in her arms. The old man pointed at the little girl and said, "She will be your future wife." He thought that the old man was just making silly stories and telling ridiculous lies. He decided to send a man to kill the little girl, so that he could prove the old man was a liar and prevent him from lying to other people. However, the man he sent was too kind and could not bring himself to kill the little girl. Instead, he just made a cut on her face.

14 years later, Wei decided to get married. His wife to be was the daughter of Wang Tai, a state official of the central government. Wang's daughter was very pretty, yet she always kept part of her face covered. Wei was understandably curious about it and asked his wife many times until she finally told him what happened. She said, "Actually it is quite distressing to talk about. One day, 14 years ago, I was out walking and, a man appeared out of nowhere and slashed my face with a knife. It wasn't a serious injury, but the resulting tiny scar just won't go away." Wei was shocked, as he recalled the moment 14 years ago when he had encountered the old man under the moon. It was only then that he finally believed that the old man really was the God who arranged marriages. Since the old man did not tell him his name, he became known simply as "The Old Man under the Moon" or in short, Yue Lao.

The Old Man under the Moon is like Cupid of Roman mythology. Cupid uses an arrow to bring couples together while Yue Lao uses a red string. In the Tang Dynasty (618 – 907), it had already become a custom to have a red string in wedding ceremonies — The red string is given to the groom's parents, to tie around the hands of the bridal couple. Gradually, in the Song Dynasty (960 – 1279), the red string was replaced by a red handkerchief and in the Qing Dynasty (1644 – 1911), it evolved again. By then, a red cloth is used, where the couple, each grasping a corner, hold each other in their arms and enter their bedroom. This practice has been retained today and many couples still carry red cloths during their wedding ceremonies.

Legend has it that, as long as Yue Lao has tied red string

around the legs of the two people, then the two of them, no matter how far apart they were and how different their family background was, would eventually get married. From this we can see that, the Chinese used to believe that marriages are arranged by fate, so the couple must support each other and never leave their partner. There is also a kind of knot called "Knot of the Common Heart", which is made by tying two simple knots together. This can be used as a wedding gift, as it signifies "tying two hearts together forever". These traditional Chinese marital values like tying two hearts together and staying together no matter what happens could really inspire current society, and remind people about the sanctity of marriage and the promises and responsibilities it entails.

Knot of the Common Heart

5 | Zhaojun the Peace Ambassador

Wang Zhaojun (50 BC – ?) is one of the four most beautiful women ever in the history of China. Since she had such a pretty face, she was naturally chosen to work in the imperial palace as a maid. One day, the emperor ordered a painter to draw portraits of the maids in the palace, so that he could use them to pick his wives. As everybody knew, it would be the turning point of a girl's life, or even her family's reputation, if she was chosen to be the queen. Therefore many maids bribed the painter, hoping that he would paint them more beautifully to catch the emperor's attention. Zhaojun saw all this and she thought that it was wrong, so she went to see the painter to tell him that he should not do so. This enraged the painter so when he painted her portrait, he intentionally added a mole on her face. Inevitably, this led to the result of her being overlooked in the selection.

Shortly after that, there was a tribe, the Huns (also known as Xiongnu), who had challenged the sovereignty and authority of the Han Court for quite some time. They came with a request of Heqin (marriage in exchange for peace). The Han emperor agreed instantly, so he decided to pick the bride from among the maids in the palace. He put up a notice declaring: "Whoever is willing to marry the Huns' leader will be treated as a princess of mine."

Zhaojun saw this and thought, "If I couldn't attract the attention of the emperor, I might have to spend my entire life in the palace as a maid. On the other hand, I could choose to marry the tribal leader in order to solve the emperor's dilemma, and at the same time preserve the peaceful state of the country." After some thought, she went to the emperor and asked him to send her over to the Huns to fulfil the requested marriage. She adapted to tribal life and because of the marriage, the Huns and the Han people lived together peacefully for the next sixty years or so. Interestingly, the Han emperor only realised how beautiful Zhaojun was after seeing her leave for the Huns, by which time, of course, it was too late to change his mind.

The image of Zhaojun holding a Pipa (a kind of Chinese musical instrument) as she set off for the Huns all alone is legendary and stays in everybody's heart. She has long been praised for her bravery in leaving her hometown and her contribution to promoting peace between the Huns and the Han. Her heroic act has touched many people so she became the subject of many literary works and the muse of numerous poets. Some wrote with a sad tone, some praised her achievements, while some, like Li Shangyin (812 – 858), wrote a poem criticising the painter in the palace. However, the majority of the works were on the issue of grievances. This is because many

Zhaojun

writers and poets saw the similarity between Zhaojun's failure to win the emperor's recognition for her pretty face, and their own failure to advance in their own careers due to their talents not being spotted. Through depicting her life in their works, writers and poets could show their feeling towards Zhaojun and also mourn the frustration of not having their talents appreciated.

The practice of Heqin made it possible for two tribes and nations to live together peacefully. Many conflicts were minimised, while the free flow of information and knowledge between the two places was beneficial to economic and cultural development. Nowadays, we are living under an unstoppable trend of globalisation. There are more and more chances for countries to co-operate and there is also an increase in the frequency of interaction between different groups and parties. Let us hope that in the future, we will all be able to live together peacefully in the world.

6 The Brotherhood of Liu-Guan-Zhang

During the final years of the Eastern Han Dynasty (25 – 220), the government was corrupt and unable to carry out any good policies. In addition to that, there were years of drought which caused famines, so the people lived very difficult lives. In the face of such a situation, Liu Bei (161 – 223) sighed. Suddenly, someone behind him shouted, "Why does a man sigh but not contribute to the country?" He turned to see the speaker, who was eight feet tall, with a head like a leopard's, standing there with a forceful presence. This man introduced himself, "I am Zhang Fei (? – 221)." The two men took an instant liking to each other and greeted each other like long lost friends, so they decided to go for some wine and more conversation.

While they were drinking, a man, nine feet tall, with very long beard, came in for a drink. Liu thought that this man looked different from ordinary people, so he decided to get to know him and invited him to join them for a drink. He went up to the man and asked for his name. The man replied, "I am Guan Yu (? – 220). In my village, there was a villain who bullied the others, I was so angry with him that I simply killed him. Since then, I have been in hiding for five years." Both Liu and Zhang respected Guan a lot. The three men felt that they shared a lot of common ideas and interests, so they decided to go to the Peach Garden (also known as Taoyuan) where they had a brotherhood ceremony to become sworn brothers.

A Brotherhood Ceremony

It was said that during the brotherhood ceremony, they had no idea who should be the eldest brother, so Zhang pointed to a tree and suggested that they could be ranked according to their speed in climbing the tree. The other two agreed. Zhang was very strong, so he was the quickest of the three. Guan was second, while Liu, who was not very strong physically, ended up the last. Zhang was so proud and happy, expecting to be the eldest brother, but at that time, Liu said, "Let's consider the growth of a tree. Obviously the root of the tree came first, then its trunk and branches and finally the tips. In this case, as the tree grows from the bottom to the top, it would be more reasonable for the person who is at the bottom part of the tree to be the eldest, and the one who is at the top to be the youngest." Upon hearing this, Zhang and Guan completely agreed, so Liu became the eldest brother amongst them.

According to the history books, the three of them made a promise to work together to form a force and protect the emperor; they would remain loyal to the royal family and would put people's interest first in their hearts. It sounded easy, but it wasn't. At that time, the royal family was very weak, and the emperor was just a young kid, so the emperor was under great pressure all the time from other generals and warlords, who were also fighting among themselves in order to gain full control of the country. Liu was a good politician, a great thinker and clever in making speeches, while Guan was a great general, as he remained calm under any conditions. As to Zhang, he was very brave and physically very strong, and thus a very good warrior. The three brothers, known as Liu-Guan-Zhang, made use of their own talents to build their forces from scratch until they were one of the three main armies occupying south-western China. One other promise they made when they became brothers, which became very famous, was the promise that even though they were not born on the same day, they aspired to die on the same day at the same time. Unfortunately because of the war, this did not come about.

This legend in addition to the fact that the period saw three great kingdoms struggling each other became one of the most interesting times in Chinese history. People were so fascinated about the stories from this period that one of the best four Chinese novels slightly embellished was written based on known facts and is known as *Romance of the Three Kingdoms* (or *Sanguo Yanyi*). The story of Liu-Guan-Zhang gained increasing legendary status and was passed on for generations.

7 | Joining the Army for Her Father – Mulan

Have you watched Mulan, the animated film produced by the Walt Disney in the late 1990s? The story is based on a Chinese legend, which is about Hua Mulan joining the army for her father. Obviously they altered parts of the story in the film to suit the audience, but if you have watched it, you will still have some understanding of the original version of the legend. Nevertheless, let's look at how it happened.

A war broke out at one of the border areas of the Middle Kingdom, where another tribe was trying to invade the country by breaking through. Under such critical circumstances, the government sent out recruitment requests one after another to gather as many soldiers as possible. Mulan saw the document identifying her aging father as a recruit, and she thought to herself, "Dad is so old that all his hair has turned white, and he is so weak, while my brother is still too young, so both of them are not suitable to serve the army. What should I do?" After thinking for a moment, an idea suddenly struck her — she could actually do it in her father's name! The next day, Mulan went to buy a horse and a piece of armour that would be essential for the war. She put them on when she got home, and everyone in her family agreed that she looked fit in the armour. Since there were no other options, her parents agreed to let her join the army.

Joining the Army for Her Father – Mulan

Due to regular practice with her father when she was young, she did very well in the war, killing numerous enemies in various battles. All sorts of merit were achieved with her outstanding performance for the army in the battlefields, and she became a "hero". After their triumphant return, everyone in the army received huge rewards from the emperor. The emperor told Mulan that she had achieved a lot and in return he would offer her a post in the state. However, she told the emperor that she was not interested in being an official; instead, she only wanted to go home to be with her parents and serve them well. The emperor was touched by her concern about her parents so he sent some men to accompany her along the journey home.

Upon arrival, she was so glad to be home again and immediately went into her room to get changed. When she came out of the room, all the men who accompanied her home were utterly surprised. They found it really difficult to believe that after being with her for over ten years, they did not realise that Mulan was actually a female!

In all these years, in addition to being a figure enjoying a heroine status due to all her merits achieved at war, Mulan is even more famous for being a good daughter to her parents. This is because the Chinese always think that filial piety should be a very high priority in one's life. Serving one's parents is understood as the most basic as well as the most important of moral acts. There are many folk songs and poems about Mulan which describe the whole story in praise of her. It would be safe to assume that the majority of Chinese people have heard about Mulan's story, and many of them will actually be able to at least recall a few lines of folk songs and poems written about her.

8 The Butterfly Lovers

In the West, the tragedy of Romeo and Juliet has long been one of the greatest stories ever told. It has also been recreated in many different forms, like dramas, operas, films, ballet, orchestra and television drama. Coincidentally, there is a story very similar in China too which has been reproduced in various forms of art. It is amazing that this story, the love story of Liang and Zhu, is still mentioned in the lyrics of some pop-songs nowadays. There is even a saying that goes like this: "If a couple wants their love to last forever, they must pay a visit to the temple of Liang."

During the Eastern Jin Dynasty (317 – 420), there was a girl called Zhu Yingtai. She was bright, and had always hoped to go to school. The problem was, at that time, girls were not allowed to go to school. The tradition back then was that girls were to stay at home, where they would learn weaving, tailoring, reading and playing musical instruments. One day, Zhu came up with an innovative idea — she dressed herself up as a boy, and begged her parents to allow her to go to school. Seeing that their daughter was so determined, they had no other options but to give in.

On her way to school in Hangzhou, Zhu met Liang Shanbo, a fellow student. They got along very well and shared many common interests and future goals between them, so in the next three years in school, they became really close friends. Zhu even developed a romantic feeling for Liang, however, since he was rather insensitive, he did not feel anything. Some time later, Zhu's father asked her to return home. Before leaving Hangzhou, she tried to fix a marriage between Liang and herself by asking him to marry "her sister". At the same time she also told the wife of their teacher that she had pretended to be a man, and asked her to relay this message to him.

After learning that Zhu was in fact a girl, he tried his best to rush to her home. Unfortunately when he arrived, he was told that her father had already agreed for her to be married to Ma Wencai, the son of the town governor. The two of them finally met, but their meeting was overwhelmed by sadness and frustration, as it

The Butterfly Lovers

was impossible for them to get married. Afterwards, he decided to leave, since there was nothing he could do to change the situation. He passed away shortly after arriving home. The news of his death finally reached Zhu, and she decided to remain loyal to him forever.

The day of marriage eventually arrived. The Ma family followed the traditional customs and sent a carriage over to the Zhu family to pick her up. On the way to the home of the Ma family, she insisted on being taken to Liang's tomb. Upon arrival, she got off the carriage, and thinking of him, tears came rolling down her face. All of a sudden, a thunderstorm came from nowhere and Liang's tomb cracked open; she seized the chance and jumped into the hole created by the gap. After jumping in the tomb closed up as it was before the arrival of her carriage. Moments later, a couple of colourful butterflies appeared from the tomb and flew away. And that was how the story ended.

This romantic story showed that traditional marriages were often determined by two major factors: one, the will of the parents; and two, the status of the two families involved in the marriage. There was nothing that Zhu could do about it so she decided to use her death to speak for herself. The story also reflected how the ancient Chinese thought about love. They believed that lovers should be buried in the same space so that the love and marriage that could not exist in the real world could carry forward into the after-life.

9 | The White Lady

Love stories are always more popular than other types of stories. There is the romance of Liang and Zhu turning into butterflies related in the previous section, and there is another love story between the White Lady and Xu Xian.

It was said that in his previous life, Xu saved the life of a white snake. After being saved, the white snake went on to become a practitioner of some magical power and finally she turned into a Jing. (A Jing is a spirit that can transform itself into something real and has magical power. The closest thing to a Jing in Western mythical creatures would be a genie.) The white snake genie transformed itself into a woman with the name Bai Suzhen (also known as the White Lady), and took a maid along with her, who was also transformed from a green snake genie. The White Lady came to look for Xu as she wanted to repay the kindness shown by him in saving her life. Unsurprisingly, the two fell in love and got married, and the White Lady became pregnant. One day, when Xu was on his way home, he came across a monk called Fahai. Fahai told him that his wife and the maid were both snake genies. Naturally, he did not believe it at all. He laughed heartily and said, "How is it possible that my wife is actually a genie?"

As Fahai was a powerful monk, it was his duty to capture

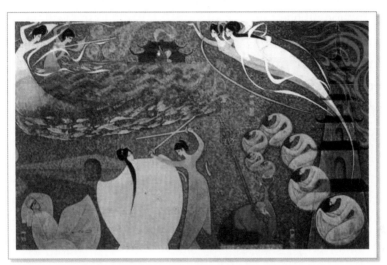

Flooding of the Jinshan Temple

all genies in the world. In order to try to lure the White Lady into a fight so that she could be captured, he first lured Xu up to the Jinshan Temple and locked him up. This enraged her and she proceeded to use her magical power to draw upon huge amount of water to flood the temple. Fahai hung his basin on the door of the temple, and started using his power to stop the water. In the midst of all these, he shouted, "You white snake! You are so brave, now you are going to fight against me?" She answered, "Now what makes you think that you are in the position to separate my husband and me?" Just as the White Lady was overpowering him and the water nearly flooded the temple completely, she suffered her labour pains. The pains were too much of a distraction for her and in the end, she was defeated. She passed the baby to her maid and ordered her to flee immediately. Fahai came up, took his basin out and captured her in his basin. After that, he locked her under the Leifeng Tower at West Lake.

Years later, her son grew up and did well in the imperial

examinations. The maid, the son and Xu came to the Leifeng Tower to hold a memorial for her. All of a sudden, the Buddha appeared and released her from her prison at the bottom of the tower. The Buddha told her to go back to the magical realm and continue her practice. She was satisfied with this last chance of seeing her husband and her son again, so she listened to the Buddha and left the human world.

Traditionally, snakes give us negative impressions but the Chinese people love the White Lady. A possible reason for this is that the White Lady and Xu were very loyal to each other and remained constant in their love. The White Lady dared to love and thus endeared her to the people. People are touched that she tried to save Xu when she knew he was in trouble even though she knew she might not be powerful enough to win against the monk.

Valuing loyalty and keeping promises between couples are highly regarded. In the above story, the White Lady and Xu provide a very good example. No matter how hard the monk tried to separate them, they remained committed to each other. This contrasts with the number of divorces in modern marriages and may provide inspiration for people nowadays.

Chapter 2
Festivals and Folklore

1 The Spring and Yuanxiao Festivals

The Spring Festival (also known as Lunar New Year or Chunjie) is on the 1st day of the 1st month in the Chinese calendar year. It is the biggest and also the most important festival for the Chinese.

During the Spring Festival, there are a few things everyone does: lighting firecrackers, placing blessings on the wall, and blessing each other. These traditional practices have been kept till today. It was said that, a monster called Nian brought about all these activities. Back in the ancient times, at the end of every year, the very hungry Nian would invade villages, killing the animals raised by families and even harming people's lives. People tried all sorts of methods to counter this threat and to expel it. Gradually people realised that it was afraid of noises and the colour red, therefore on the New Year's Eve, everyone wrote blessings on red paper and placed them on their front doors, and lit firecrackers to produce noise. That turned out to be successful and everyone was happily greeting each other and wishing each other the best of luck for the coming year. This became a custom and was passed along for generations since then.

The Chinese character "Nian" itself means that crops are ready to be harvested. It is a combination of two single characters, "grains" and "thousand", so the blend of the two characters means a very rich harvest. In the old days, after a year's hard work in the fields, people would prepare wine and delicious food for a rich feast with the family to celebrate the year's harvest and the arrival of a new year, so this was the most important and the happiest day in a year. Eventually it evolved into an important festival.

In different parts of China, the celebrations might differ slightly, but they all have a common theme: See off the old and welcome the new. Nowadays, before the Lunar New Year, families are busy stocking up on special foods for the New Year and decorating their homes so that they would look new to welcome a new year. On New Year's Day, people will wear new clothes to visit relatives and friends to give them blessings. In cities and towns, some people queue up to visit temples, some take part in carnivals, others perform dragon dances and in most places, there are fireworks displays.

In the 1st month of the Chinese calendar year, except for the Chinese New Year, there is another festival called the Yuanxiao

Yuanxiao lanterns

Festival. It is on the 15th day of the month. In the past, people hung paper lanterns and everyone went out at night to look at the lanterns on this day. As you can imagine, the sight of different lanterns on the street at night is a very beautiful scene. Nowadays, with the increasing influence of Western culture, and probably because of the beautiful and romantic scene of lanterns as well, another meaning has been added to the Yuanxiao Festival — it is now also known as the Chinese Valentine's Day.

Yuanxiao Festival actually started way back in the Western Han Dynasty (206 BC – 23 AD). At that time, there was a maid in the imperial palace named Yuanxiao. She felt bored and homesick being trapped in the imperial palace, so she wanted to commit suicide by jumping down a well. A man who was very famous for his intelligence, named Dongfang Shuo, learnt this and felt sorry for Yuanxiao, so he tried to think of a way to help her. A few days later, he dressed up as a fortune-teller and wandered around in the town. People came up to him and asked for help. Everyone got the same response — they would be burnt by fire on the 15th day of the first month. This made them panic. The news got through to the emperor, and the emperor decided to ask the most intelligent man — yes, Dongfang himself — for a solution.

Dongfang told the emperor that the God of Fire loved dumplings a lot. Therefore he suggested that the emperor could ask Yuanxiao to offer some dumplings to the God of Fire and worship him. Then everyone should go out on to the streets that night, and light numerous red lanterns on every house and every street. He explained that the city would appear to be on fire, if looked down from heaven, and this would confuse the God of Fire and make him think that he had already set the fire. The emperor agreed with this and ordered everyone to do as he suggested.

That day finally came, and the city was fully alive that night, everyone was wandering around the streets and Yuanxiao got a chance to meet up with her family too. The night passed peacefully as well. The emperor was delighted and he ordered to keep this ritual forever on this day of every year from then on.

Gradually, in time, more activities have been added rather to just appreciating lanterns. For example, riddles are tied to the lanterns, so while appreciating the beautiful lanterns, people can also try to solve the riddles. Apart from the lanterns, another thing which must be present on that day is a kind of dumplings made of flour. These dumplings are in a round shape, which resemble the shape of a full moon. (In the Chinese calendar year, it is always a full moon on the 15th day of each month.) The Chinese believe that a full moon symbolises the reunion of a family, so on that day, every family member will sit together and enjoy the dumplings.

2 The Qingming and Hanshi Festivals

There are numerous pieces of Chinese literature produced based on the topic of the Qingming Festival. In those works, Qingming is always described as a day full of sadness, and most of the time it is a rainy day, when the rain is light and mild. Also, people often visit the cemetery on that day. However, in the ancient times, Qingming (meaning "pure brightness" if translated directly) had nothing to do with visiting the cemetery or remembering the ancestors. It was just one of the 24 solar terms in the Chinese calendar year where it represented the time for farmers to plough and to plant the seeds. It is usually on a day in the second or the third month of the Chinese calendar year when spring arrives.

So how is Qingming eventually became linked to visiting the cemeteries? Visiting cemeteries was actually the traditional thing to do during the Hanshi Festival. The Hanshi itself has a story behind it. During the Spring and Autumn Period (770 BC – 476 BC), Jie Zhitui followed the prince of the State of Jin, Chong'er, who went into exile. One day, they got lost and were trapped in the mountains, they had no food left and there was no one passing by to offer help. Jie saw that the prince was extremely hungry, so he decided to cut off a piece of meat from his own thigh to cook as food for the prince.

After 19 years of exile, the prince finally returned to Jin and became the king. He wanted to reward Jie for his kindness and generosity, but Jie did not want any rewards, he only wanted to be with his elderly mother to look after her well, so he moved to live in the woods with her. The king was not impressed when the messenger told him that Jie did not want to be a government official; he insisted that Jie come and work for him. Upon hearing that the government officials were after him, Jie decided to hide, so he carried his mother on his back and went deep into the mountains. Again, the news came to the king that his invitation had failed because Jie was hidden deep in the mountains.

At this point, the king decided to force him out of the mountains, so he ordered his men to set fire to the mountains and burn down everything until he came out. Of course, Jie remained unwilling to come out, at last there was nothing he could do but climb a tree in an attempt to escape the fire but was burned to death. The king heard about this and started to regret his previous decision. Consequently, he ordered that from then on, no fire was allowed to be lit on this day ever again. This day became known as the Hanshi Festival, and was always one or two days before Qingming. Since the two days were so close to each other, people simply combined them. Nowadays, the Chinese almost never recognise the Hanshi Festival; instead, they maintain the habit of visiting the cemeteries on Qingming Festival.

During Qingming Festival, a lot of Chinese, even those who are living overseas, try to get back to their hometown to visit their ancestors' tombs, bringing bunches of fresh flowers, fruits, wine, joss-sticks and other materials for worship along with them. Visitors of the tombs will not only make a prayer to their ancestors but they will also clean the graves by removing weeds and cleaning the headstones, and then offering sacrifices for to worship the deceased.

Respecting and treating those who are older than you well is an important thing to do according to traditional Chinese moral values. This attitude extends towards those who have passed away. The idea of attending the funeral rites of parents and worshipping them on important days is still very strong these days, although many people cannot really follow them because of the constraints of the busy working schedules in the modern world. However, at the very least, whenever it's Qingming Festival, most Chinese will go to the cemetery to visit their ancestors' tombs and pay their respect.

Visiting the Cemetery

3 | The Dragon Boat Festival

Nowadays, when it's close to the 5th day of the 5th month in the Chinese calendar year, rice dumplings will be found in most food shops. Various ingredients can be used to fill the dumplings. In the old days, there were also games that involved the dumplings. There were races for unwrapping the dumplings (the leaves used for wrapping this kind of dumpling could not be eaten), and there were also competitions for people to shoot the dumplings from a distance. As for the dragon boat race, an international boat race event is held in Hong Kong annually during the Dragon Boat Festival. Top teams from all over the world will come over to participate. On the day of the race, coloured flags will be put up, together with the sounds of drums and the shouts of athletes, a very lively atmosphere will be produced. In the race, everyone must row according to the rhythm of the drum, so rowing not only makes one stronger physically, but it also builds up team spirit.

There is apparently no definitive answer to the question of how, and when did people first started to celebrate the Dragon Boat Festival. The legend began with a patriotic poet called Qu Yuan (340 BC – 278 BC) in the Warring States Period (475 BC – 221 BC). The most famous work of his is surely a poem entitled *Li Sao* — the longest sentimental poem in the Chinese classical literature. It is a very touching piece of work, in which he had shown a very deep passion for his country. Qu was a government official, although throughout his life he was being attacked scathingly by other officials, he remained true to himself all the time and he stuck to what he believed to be good for the country; also, he often criticised selfish people who put themselves above all else. His persistence in achieving the good and his attack the dark side of bad people are the most loved aspects of the poem. Moreover, his courage in offering honest suggestions without thinking about his own life is also well-respected by future generations.

With the outstanding ability to speak and to think honestly the king made Qu a major official when he was young. He had been a very loyal official in the State of Chu. At that time, it was a turbulent period, with Qin being the strongest state of all. He was constantly making wise suggestions to the king, hoping that the state could be strengthened, so they would be able to resist the ambitious Qin. However, implementing his ideas would affect the benefit of the nobles and other powerful persons, so they started making false accusations against him. The king then started to keep him at a distance and eventually sent him into exile. Shortly afterwards, Qin invaded Chu, and Qin easily won the war. He sensed that the end of Chu was near, and that his aspirations would never come true, so he committed suicide by drowning himself in the river out of frustration.

When the people of Chu learned about this, everyone rushed to the riverside, but of course it was already too late. Some of them mourned his death, others cried. In order to ensure that his body would remain intact, people rowed boats on the river and produced noises with drums and gongs so as to scare the fish in the river away. They also threw food into the river so that the fish would feed on those instead of Qu's body. This was the origin of the dragon boat race and dumplings.

Qu chased his dreams all through his life. In the choice between maintaining his belief and risking his life, he chose the former. Even though he came across a lot of obstacles in the process, he always faced them positively.

Dragon boat race

4 The Qixi Festival

In the Chinese myths, the Queen Mother of the West (also known as Wangmu Niangniang), who was the daughter of the Heavenly King, had a granddaughter called the Sister Seventh (also known as Qijie) . She was clever, and her greatest skill was weaving, thus she had a nickname called the Weaving Maid (also known as Zhinü). One day, she went down to the human world to enjoy herself, where she came across an ordinary man called the Cowherd (also known as Niulang). The two of them loved each other at first sight, and they got married and lived together happily.

That was until the news reached the Heavenly King. After he learned what had happened, he was outraged. On the 7th day of the 7th month, he ordered the army in the Heaven to go and bring the Weaving Maid back. The soldiers did so and escorted her back to Heaven. However the Cowherd did not want to let go so easily, so he tried all his might to follow the soldiers from Heaven. He was getting closer and closer, until suddenly the Queen Mother of the West appeared, with a hairpin in her hand. She waved her arm and drew a Heavenly River with great roaming waves with the hairpin, separating the Cowherd from the Weaving Maid and the soldiers. As a result, the two lovers could only see each other from the two sides of the river.

Meeting at the Heavenly River

Days went by, the Cowherd and the Weaving Maid still felt deeply in love with each other, even though they were separated physically by the Heavenly River. Gradually, the Queen Mother of the West was touched by the pair's persistence in love, and she decided to allow them to meet each other once a year, on the 7th day of the 7th month of each year. On that night every year, magpies would gather at the Heavenly River. They would organise themselves in rows to form a bridge for the two lovers, so that they could reach each other.

People were deeply touched by this love story. Therefore on that day each year, they worship the Weaving Maid, and that was the origin of the Qixi (meaning "7th night" if translated directly) Festival. On this day, girls will pray to her and make wishes — every girl wanted to be as skilful in weaving as the Weaving Maid.

On the night of Qixi, there used to be a race, where girls would weave under the moonlight; the quicker they could weave, the higher chance they had of becoming a very skilful weaver.

Apart from the Weaving Maid's exceptional weaving skills, the Cowherd and the Weaving Maid's belief in love and their bravery in making the seemingly impossible to become possible has been passed on for generations. On that night, in addition to praying for the Weaving Maid to pass them her weaving skills, girls will also pray to be married to their lovers and enjoy a happy marriage. Obviously, such a love story has touched a lot of people, especially those who write well. One of the most famous pieces was written by Qin Guan (1049 – 1100) in the Northern Song Dynasty (960 – 1127), which mainly talked about the sadness felt by the two as they were separated from each other. At the end of that piece, there is a very famous line — If the love between a couple is long-lasting, any obstacles will fall away — for as the author pointed out, true love can defeat the boundaries of time and space.

The story of the Cowherd and the Weaving Maid is almost as romantic as it gets, but this romance actually reflected the restrictions on freedom of love back in the old days, a traditional society where there were all sorts of rules and regulations established by the elderly in limiting the freedom and possibilities of free love.

5 The Mid-Autumn Festival

There is a very interesting story behind the Mid-Autumn Festival. It was said that Hou Yi (Remember him? The one who almost shot down all the suns.) got some pills from the Queen Mother of the West (the grandmother of the Weaving Maid in the previous story) that would give him eternal life. One day, as he was out, his wife Chang'e took the pills. All of a sudden, she started losing weight, and finally she was so light that she was floating in the air. She was flying higher and higher, and the next thing she knew, she was at the palace on the moon! It was because she took the pills without letting Hou know about it, so the punishment for her was to be alone on the moon forever. Since then, people always worshipped the moon on Mid-Autumn Festival, hoping to see Chang'e and also make her feel less lonely up there on the moon.

Flying to the moon

In fact, there is another source, which stretched back further in time, pointing out that the Mid-Autumn Festival actually originated from a habit in the past called Qiu Si, in which the people worshipped the moon. In the ancient times, nearly everyone worked on farms. As the harvest of crops depended heavily on climate and seasonal changes, people would usually prepare good food on the day of Qiu Si to offer thanks to the Heaven for giving them rich harvests for the year. As the harvests usually came in the autumn, the act of gratitude was usually performed in autumn too, hence the Mid-Autumn Festival. There were also series of celebrations held in that period as well. The Mid-Autumn Festival can actually be read literally: It is on the 15th day in the 8th month of the lunar year, which is in the middle of autumn. In the past, people observed that the moon was always the roundest on that night, therefore actions like worshipping the moon was held on that day. Gradually, it evolved into the present habit of enjoying and admiring the full moon.

Food is always crucial to the Chinese people, and there is no exception here. Pomelo is a popular fruit during the Mid-Autumn Festival, but mooncake is even more popular. The word "mooncake" first appeared in the history books in the Song Dynasty (960 – 1279). It was said that during the Yuan Dynasty (1271 – 1368), there was someone called Liu Bowen who wanted a revolution, and was looking for those who shared his thoughts. He came up with a brilliant trick, where he started a rumour saying that a plague was about to come. He also added that people must eat Shaobing (a kind of sesame seed cake) to avoid catching the plague. As a result, everyone rushed to buy them. When they got home, cut open the Shaobing, and were about to eat it, they saw a piece of paper hidden inside. There was a line on the paper saying "The revolution starts on the 15th of August." Eventually, the revolution to overturn the Yuan Dynasty started that night and was a great success because everyone got the message and acted together.

Nowadays, the production of mooncakes is a very complicated process. Every step from baking, packaging and naming are all closely monitored and carefully prepared. There are many different kinds of mooncakes, like the traditional ones made from lotus seed mash, modern ones made from green bean, even snowy ones (the outer skin is iced) and the more outrageous ice-cream ones. In people's minds, the full moon represents the completeness of the whole family, and mooncakes are also round in shape, therefore they resemble the full moon. To the Chinese, who traditionally emphasized family togetherness and the close relationship between family members, mooncakes and the full moon are all the more meaningful.

On the day of Mid-Autumn Festival, families could enjoy the moon while eating mooncakes and pomelos and spend some precious time together. That is why people place more significance on this special day. For those who live abroad, they will also look at the moon on that night while thinking about their family, as they believe that, by looking at the same moon, even if the family members are not physically together, they may somehow be able to connect with each other mentally through the moon.

6 The 24 Solar Terms and the Chinese Calendar

Astronomy and mathematics have always been important to the ancient Chinese. They accumulated an impressive store of knowledge about the universe, and used it to explain its existence and events. In the Chinese calendar, there are 24 Jieqi (specific stages) in a year in which there are minor climatic changes ("minor" in relation to its preceding or following stage). Each of those stages is marked by a term on a single day, indicating what the change is. For example, one of the 24 Jieqi is called Dongzhi (Winter Solstice in solar terms), on that day, the daylight hours are always the shortest in the year. The Winter Solstice is usually on the 22nd of December in the Western calendar too.

In fact, the 24 Jieqi are drawn according to the position of the earth at various times during its revolution around the sun. A revolution around the sun by the earth is a 360 degrees' turn, dividing it by 24 equates to 15 degrees, and so each stage is marked by a 15 degree turn along the path of revolution. The establishment of the 24 Jieqi was hugely beneficial to agricultural activities, and so they appeared in the Chinese calendar from very early times. As a year in the Western calendar is also the time taken for the Earth to go around the sun once, the 24 Jieqi could match the Western calendar as well.

The names of the four seasons Chun, Xia, Qiu and Dong (Spring, Summer, Autumn and Winter respectively in English) first appeared in China about 3,000 years ago. The ancient Chinese started identifying Dongzhi and Xiazhi (Summer Solstice), by standing a bamboo stick upright, and then measuring the length of its shadow at noon. They observed that the length of the shadow was the shortest on Summer Solstice, and that the daylight hours were the longest, which was the opposite for Winter Solstice. Upon more observation, it was discovered that there were 2 days in which the daytime was exactly as long as night-time; these two days were in the middle of Spring and Autumn, so the 2 days were named as Chunfen (Spring Equinox) and Qiufen (Autumn Equinox). Later, Lichun (The Beginning of Spring), Lixia (The Beginning of Summer), Liqiu (The Beginning of Autumn) and Lidong (The Beginning of Winter) were added, the 8 days marked Spring, Summer, Autumn and Winter. In the Western Han Dynasty (206 BC – 23 AD), the 8 stages were further developed into the 24 Jieqi, and they have been maintained till now.

The four seasons

As China is huge, climatic changes differ in different regions. The 24 Jieqi were measured in the area at the lower end of the Yellow River, so naturally they reflected the climatic changes of that region. The latitudes and the geographical landscape are different in other parts of China, so it is less accurate when applied to other regions. Nevertheless, it was a proof of the Chinese people's high intelligence back then.

In ancient times, whenever a new dynasty was established in place of the previous one, a new calendar would be announced to indicate the beginning of a new era. Finally in the Yuan Dynasty (1271 – 1368), a major breakthrough in the development of the Chinese calendar came in the form of Shoushi Li created by Guo Shoujing (1231 – 1316). At that time, the emperor appointed Guo, who was an expert in astronomy, to compile a new calendar. He believed that for the calendar to be reliable, the measuring apparatus must be very advanced, so he designed some new apparatus and improved the old ones, and he set up 27 observatory stations around the country. After carrying out a full-scaled investigation and detailed calculation, Shoushi Li was created successfully in the year 1280. It is also the most accurate calendar, as it adapted the advantages of other calendars, and was created with scientific calculations and theories backing it up. According to Shoushi Li, a year is 365.2425 days long and that is exactly the same as the calendar we are now using, except that it was introduced 300 years before the Gregorian Calendar — the calendar currently in use.

Different kinds of calendars have been used in different parts of the world at different times. The three most important ones were the solar calendar, lunar calendar and a combination of both. The solar calendar considers the time taken for the earth to complete a revolution around the sun as a year, and is the most widely-used calendar in the modern world. In this calendar, there is an intercalary month once every 4 years where there is an extra day added in February. The lunar calendar considers the time taken for the moon to complete a revolution around the earth as a month and was used by Muslims — but these days, only a minority of the Arab world still use the Islamic Calendar. The Chinese mostly used the calendar which combined both the solar calendar and lunar calendar. As it was first created in the Xia Dynasty (21st century BC – 16th century BC), it was also called Xia Calendar (or Xia Li). As farmers followed this calendar, it was also called Agricultural Calendar (or Nong Li). There are 354 days in a year in this calendar, meaning there is a deviation of 11 days compared to the most accurate calculation of 365 days a year, so in every 19 years, 7 intercalary months are added in order to maintain its accuracy. When we look at a Chinese calendar nowadays, it is common to notice that the solar calendar and the agricultural calendar are both shown, which means that the agricultural calendar is still widely observed and followed.

7 | The Interesting Story of the 12 Zodiac Animals

We all know cats chase rats when cats see them, but have you ever wondered why? Why is it not other small animals but rats? The Chinese had an explanation for this. When the world was first formed, the Heavenly King announced to all kinds of animals that they could go to the Heavenly Palace the next day, and that the 12 earliest kinds of animals to arrive would be chosen to represent a year, once in each cycle which consisted of twelve years. The cat and the rat were great friends back then, and they both wanted to be chosen as a representative, so the cat asked the rat to wake it up so that they could go to the Heavenly Palace together. The rat agreed,

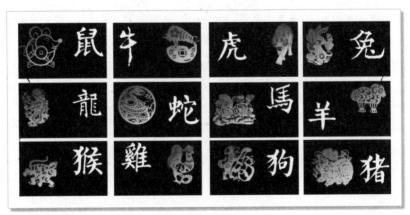

Zodiac Animals

however it sneaked out the next morning and went by itself, leaving the cat sleeping alone.

On the way, the rat met the ox, so it jumped on the ox and they travelled together. When they were just about to arrive at the Heavenly Palace, the rat jumped off suddenly and sprinted to the destination, reaching it ahead of the ox. Later on, other animals, including the pig, arrived. Then the king asked the pig to list the animals in the order that they arrived. On the list, the pig put itself in the first place, and the king was angry about this. He pointed to the pig and said, "You are too selfish!" The king put the pig at the end of the cycle as a punishment, and ruled that the other 11 animals to be ranked in the order of their arrival at the Heavenly Palace. The order is as follows: the rat, the ox, the tiger, the rabbit, the dragon, the snake, the horse, the goat, the monkey, the rooster, the dog and the pig. Of course, it was too late when the cat woke up for it to be included. Since then, cats and rats became enemies.

When you tell others which animal year you belong to, that person could probably guess your age! This is because the animals are in that particular order as mentioned above, and they repeat only every 12 years. Therefore by correctly estimating your age range, in addition to the knowledge of the animal you belong to, it would be enough to accurately tell your age. One of the cycles started in the year 2008, so people born in that year would belong to the year of the rat, people born in 2009 would belong to the year of the ox and so on, until 2019. Then in 2020, the cycle starts all over again from the rat. From this, you can then calculate which animal year you belong to as well.

For the fortune-tellers and the Fengshui specialists, the Dizhi is used instead of the 12 zodiac animals to calculate years and ages. The Dizhi sounds to be more sophisticated than using the animals, because it is more difficult for the general public to understand those words. However, they are actually the same thing, as both the animals and Dizhi consist of a cycle of 12, each representing a year respectively. This is an interesting idea from the people in the past, which made the whole thing sound a lot less serious and a lot more interesting. It did not come from any particular person, thus showing the fantastic creativity and imagination of the ordinary people.

Many people look deeply into the fate and the characteristics of the animal year that they belong to, and use various methods and materials to predict how lucky one will be in a year. This is quite similar to the Western zodiac signs to a certain extent. Basically if you believe in them, then there are all sorts of these calculations and predictions; on the other hand, if you don't believe them at all, then they are all simply superstitions. Come to think of it, there are only 12 representative animals and there are so many people who belong to each of those animals, so how is it possible that so many people share the same characteristics and have the same fate?

8 | Yin-Yang and the Five Elements

The Eight Trigrams (or Ba Gua) is a set of meaningful symbols from ancient China, which was widely-used in fortune-telling. Fu Xi was thought to be the one who created it. Each Trigram is symbolized by three Yao (Symbol), and there are two fundamental symbols, namely the Yin "- -" and the Yang "—". So there are eight possible different combinations in arranging the three symbols, and thus the Eight Trigrams. Later on, the combination of any two trigrams together results in 64 possible variations, known as the 64 Hexagrams. Besides being used in mathematics, the Hexagrams are used to calculate occurrences of stability and change, and to predict the future.

The Book of Changes (also known as *Yi Jing*) attempts to discover the law of life and the universe. It describes two cosmological forces, called Yin and Yang, which are derived from the Supreme Pole (also known as Taiji). The relationship is illustrated in the well-known diagram of the Supreme Pole, a

The Eight Trigrams

circle where Yin occupies one and Yang the other half. The ancient thinkers stated that everything was regulated by the pattern of Yin-Yang, which was why Yin-Yang symbols were used to show the pattern of things at first, and gradually they were used to predict how things change too. At the beginning, the idea of Yin-Yang came from nature. It originally referred to places the sunshine could reach and those that sunshine could not reach, therefore things that faced the sun were Yang while the others were Yin. In the Western Zhou Dynasty (1066 BC – 771 BC), the idea of Yin-Yang grew into a concept of pairing up. Therefore in astronomy, Yin-Yang is the moon and the sun; in climate, it is cold and hot; in directions, it is down and up; in form, it is soft and hard. There are so many more that it is not possible to list them all, but some examples are earth and heaven, night and day, dark and light, water and fire, death and life and so on.

In China, "5" is the most commonly-used number by people in all aspects of life, so things would usually be divided into 5 categories, for example there are 5 main body organs, 5 tastes, and 5 basic notes in music. There are also 5 elements: metal, wood, water, fire, and earth. These 5 substances are often seen in daily lives, so they are used to explain the beginning of everything. This is further developed into a theory of relationship between the 5 elements, where one element is beneficial to another one, and the same element would suppress a different element. The beneficial relationship is as follows: wood is beneficial to fire, fire is beneficial to earth, earth is beneficial to metal, metal is beneficial to water, and water is beneficial to wood. On the other hand, the relationship of suppression looks like this: water suppresses fire, fire suppresses metal, metal suppresses wood, wood suppresses earth, and finally earth suppresses water.

The 5 elements not only play a big role in our daily lives, they also have a role in naming new-born babies. When we are born, we all have our own Bazi (the date and time of our birth); different birth periods are associated with the 5 elements. So for example, when a baby is said to be "lacking wood out of the 5 elements", that means its birth time does not have anything that relates to "wood". Therefore in the ancient times, when parents or the elderly in the village named this baby, they would try their best to put the element of "wood" into the name of the baby, or used a character that consists of "wood" as a component of the name. They believed that in this way, the gap of "wood" would be filled and the loss of a particular aspect of the 5 elements would be balanced out.

From this method of naming a baby, we can tell that the ancient Chinese believed that fate was decided by the Heaven (as normally we can not control the time of birth of a baby), and they hoped that through naming, they could alter the fate of a person.

Chapter 3

Scenic Spots and Historic Sites

1 The Yellow River

Being the birthplace of the Chinese, the Yellow River has featured in various poems written by different poets. Some focused on its speedy and forceful flow of water, such as the renowned poet Li Bai (701 – 762). In one of his famous poems, he made an analogy between the fast-flowing Yellow River and a person's transitory personal extravagance. He wrote that fame and riches were just temporary, so we should not chase after these things in our lives. Another famous poet, by the name of Wang Zhihuan (688 – 742), described the broad yet stark environment along parts of the Yellow River in one of his poems creating an abstract vision of the river in readers' minds.

In the ancient times, the Yellow River was known as "the River" or "the Huge River". Since the river runs through the Loess Plateau (also known as Huangtu Plateau) and constantly washes away sand and clay from the plateau, the water is yellow in colour. In the Tang Dynasty (618 – 907), the river was eventually given the name the Yellow River (also known as Huang He). The Yellow River starts from Qinghai Province and passes through 9 provinces including Sichuan, Gansu, Ningxia, Inner Mongolia, Shaanxi, Shanxi, Henan and Shandong, and finally converges and pours into the Bohai Sea. It is 5,494 kilometres long, and stretches over a very

The Yellow River

large area of land, covering a staggering 750,000 square kilometres.

The Yellow River runs through various landscapes like plateaux, valleys and plains. Archaeologists discovered evidence of Lantian Man (a kind of ancient human) living in valleys along the Yellow River as early as the Paleolithic Period. All through the thousands of years, areas along the Yellow River has contributed greatly to the brilliance of the Chinese civilisation, therefore the Yellow River is also seen as the cradle for the entire culture.

There is a very rich civilisation and culture along the Yellow River. Numerous archaeological discoveries like the Peiligang Culture, Yangshao Culture, and Longshan Culture prove that, in the years around 6,000 BC, people living in areas along the Yellow River had already entered the Neolithic Period. Fishing, farming and raising animals were the main activities for people to make a living.

There are also some mythical legends around those regions. For example, there was the Yan Emperor (people called him Yan Di, also known as Shennong Shi) who made major discoveries in medicine and developed advanced farming systems. There was also the Yellow Emperor (people called him Huang Di) who invented the "Car Guide" or "Sinan Car" (which evolved into a compass later), characters and arithmetic. It was said that China began its rise during the times when these two kings were alive. Therefore, they were the ancestors of the race as a whole and the Chinese call themselves "Yan-Huang's descendants".

2 | The Yangtze River

Apart from the Yellow River, another long river to the south of it passes through mountains and canyons and flows to the east, and it is called Chang Jiang. (Literally it means the "Long River"; "Yangtze River" is a name which foreigners would also recognise.) It stretches from the Tibetan Plateau, and its starting point is Tuotuo River, where the water actually came from the melting of a huge amount of snow and ice that were originally on top of the snowy mountains. It runs eastwards through Qinghai, Tibet, Yunnan, Sichuan, Chongqing, Hubei, Hunan, Jiangxi, Anhui and Jiangsu, and finally into the East China Sea.

The Yangtze River is about 6,300 kilometres long, covering an area of 1.8 million square kilometres. It is the longest river in China, and is also the third longest river in the world. There are different names for different sections of the Yangtze River: the part across the Qinghai Plateau is called the Tongtian River; further downstream, it is called the Jinsha River; in the Sichuan basin, it is known as the Chuan River; in the Han Jiang Plateau it is called the Jing River; downwards from that is what is normally known as the "Yangtze River".

As the Yangtze River is so long, you can imagine there are plenty of natural views and also many historical sites. The best view

The Yangtze River

can be found at the Three Gorges: Qutang Gorge, Wu Gorge and Xiling Gorge. The Three Gorges start at the Baidi Cheng and end at the Nanjin Pass at Yichang, totalling a length of 193 kilometres. In this section, visitors can witness the extreme steepness of the Qutang Gorge, the beauty of the 12 peaks at the Wu Gorge and the surging waters at the Xiling Gorge. In addition to the Three Gorges, there are other popular sites as well, for example, there is an ancient pathway of about 50 kilometres long, which was created by digging in the steep cliff along the river. In the past, when people wished to travel from one side of the mountain to the other, travelling on this kind of pathway along the cliff was the only way to do so.

The Yangtze River provides adequate water resources for farming activities along the river. And, ferries can carry passengers and transport goods across the river, which promotes economic development in the region. The Three Gorges Dam has become the largest electricity generator in the world for the usage of water power, although sacrifices have to be made for the completion of this project, where some historical sites and natural views have been flooded and destroyed forever.

The cradle of Chinese civilisation — the Yellow River — provided a platform for the rich development of Chinese culture, and Yan-Huang's descendants are always very proud of that. The most important industry in the ancient Chinese economy, farming, also benefited from the water supply of the Yangtze River, which brought economic prosperity to the region.

3 The East and West Mountains

A famous traveller in the Ming Dynasty (1369 – 1644), Xu Xiake (1586 – 1641), once said, "After you have been to the Five Sacred Mountains (also known as Wu Yue), you will not want to visit any other mountains." The five mountains are Tai Shan, Hua Shan, Heng Shan, Heng Shan (same pronunciation but with different characters) and Song Shan. Based on their geographical locations, Tai Shan is also known as the East Mountain, Hua Shan as the West Mountain, Heng Shan as the South Mountain, another Heng Shan as the North Mountain, and Song Shan as the Middle Mountain.

Tai Shan, with a height of 1,545 metres, is situated in the eastern part of the Shandong Province. It is the supreme one out of the five mountains. It is said that if one goes to Yuhuang Peak and looks down at the land below, one will get a feeling of being above everything. In Chinese history, Tai Shan has always been an important mountain because emperors from different dynasties always came to perform a ceremony called Fengshan, while the literati also came and produced many works about it.

Fengshan is a ceremony where the emperor worships Heaven and Earth. This is an action to show the emperor's ability to rule a country, and is also a chance for him to pray to the Heaven for good luck and the continuance of the prosperous state of the country. At that time, only the emperor was allowed to do so, because the emperor is also called Tianzi (Son of Heaven). It was said that during the Xia, Shang and Zhou Dynasties (21st century BC – 771 BC), 72 kings had been to Tai Shan to do so. After that, the First Emperor of Qin (259 BC – 210 BC) unified China. He and

Tai Shan

other emperors after him followed their predecessors to Fengshan here.

Tai Shan does not only have various peaks, but it also has streams in between the peaks. The streams run irregularly, forming random intersections; in some areas, there are even waterfalls. The East Stream, Middle Stream and West Stream are the three most famous streams. They flow from the top of the mountain down the steep cliff, making very unique views. Many poets used Tai Shan to express the importance of the value of human life and the pursuance of a spiritually healthy inner self, just like the way the peaks of Tai Shan have stood tall for ages and ages.

Hua Shan, on the other hand, is famous for its steepness. It is 2,154 metres tall, which is just shorter than Heng Shan. When you go up the Yuntai Peak on Hua Shan, you come across a very dangerous path called "Master Lao Plough Channel". Rumour has it that it was created by Laozi (600 BC – 470 BC) and his plough. In the old times, many workers fell off the cliff while building the path and one day Laozi was riding on his ox and passing along this path. At the bottom of the mountain he noticed that there was a great sense of foreboding. After some investigations, he realised that it was due to the injuries and death of workers working there, so he used an iron plough to open up a path through the mountains for people to pass easily by. After that, he placed the iron plough at the back of the huge rock at the cliff. To repay his kindness and generosity, the people dug a cave dedicated especially to worshipping him.

Hua Shan is located at the south of the Shaanxi Province. The uniquely high and steep cliffs are its landmark. At one point, people will be surrounded by cliffs from all sides, where there is an iron chain connecting two of the cliffs at their tops; they look like a footbridge from the Heaven. There are three words — Hui Xin Shi — carved on the wall of the cliff, suggesting that the weak and cowardly should turn around and leave. After passing this, people will then encounter one of the steepest cliffs of the mountain. Here, there is only a tiny crack in the stones, which is just enough for one person to stand on. To proceed, visitors must hold on tight to the iron chain and carefully place their feet on the stones, moving on slowly, step by step, so that they can safely climb up the peak. There are a lot more other similar steep cliffs and dangerous places here, which have successfully attracted many visitors and adventurers to come and be challenged.

4 | The Yellow Mountain

According to legends, the Yellow Emperor (also known as Huang Di) went up a mountain to achieve eternal life. An emperor in the Tang Dynasty (618 – 907), Xuanzong, named the mountain the Yellow Mountain (also known as Huang Shan) so as to commemorate the Yellow Emperor. It is located in the southern part of the Anhui Province, in an area that is about 40 kilometres long and 30 kilometres wide.

Most of the best scenery occupies an area of 154 square kilometres, known as "the Five Hundred Miles Yellow Mountain". In this section, there are many peaks, with 36 large ones and 36 smaller ones: Lianhua Feng, Tiandu Feng, and Guangming Ding are the three main peaks. Remember the saying at the beginning of the previous section? Actually there is a sentence to follow it, so the whole quote is: "After you have been to the Five Sacred Mountains, you will not want to visit any other mountains; but if you have been to the Yellow Mountain, you will not even want to visit the Five Sacred Mountains." Therefore, the Yellow Mountain has been given the title "the World's Most Special Mountain".

What make the Yellow Mountain so special? — Pine trees, strange rocks, a sea of clouds and numerous hot springs. The pine trees that grow along the cliff, are usually strong and stand upright, and the most famous pine tree is the one on Yuping Feng. The tree has two branches, which look like a pair of open arms welcoming tourists from everywhere. The strange rocks, come in all kinds of different shapes, on the cliff, in deep valleys, and just

The Yellow Mountain

about everywhere. They have all experienced thousands of years of erosion by natural processes like wind and rain, so each piece of rock is unique.

The Yellow Mountain has rainy days throughout the year, and most of the time, is surrounded by fog. Sometimes, it is soft and floats around, while other times it compacts and creates a very grand scene for tourists. Finally, the hot springs are famous for medical purposes. It was said that the Yellow Emperor once bathed there, after that, his white beard turned black, meaning he became young again! A story from the Tang Dynasty (618 – 907) says that there was once a government official who was troubled by pains in his joints. None of the doctors he visited could cure him but when he bathed in the hot springs the pain was completely gone.

With its various spectacular scenes, the Yellow Mountain has always provided a platform for travellers to admire China's beauty. In 1985, it was rated as one of the top 10 natural sites for tourism. In 1990, UNESCO even included the Yellow Mountain as one of its recommended natural heritage sites. So, a visit to the Yellow Mountain should not be missed.

5 The West Lake and Tai Hu

Su Dongpo (1037 – 1101), a very famous Chinese poet, once wrote a poem to praise the beauty of the West Lake (also known as Xi Hu), where he used Xizi (Xizi refers to Xi Shi, who is one of the four greatest beauties of China) as a metaphor for the West Lake. This has given the West Lake a nickname — Xizi Hu. No matter whether it is a sunny day or a rainy day, it is always beautiful.

The West Lake is located at Hangzhou, one of the ancient capitals of China. Hangzhou began to grow as a metropolitan city during the Sui Dynasty (581 – 618) after completion of the Great Canal linking the north and the south. Together with Suzhou, they were the best places to live in the country. There was even a saying that goes like this: "There's heaven in the sky, and there's Su-Hang on the earth." So you can tell how prestigious Hangzhou was to the people back then. During the Yuan Dynasty (1271 – 1368), the great Italian traveller Marco Polo (1254 – 1324) praised Hangzhou as the most magnificent and beautiful city in the world. Undoubtedly though, the West Lake is the main reason why people think Hangzhou is so unique.

The water of the West Lake is clear and shows the reflections of the mountains nearby, and there are poplar and willow trees along the path on both sides. In addition to that, the whole place is

The West Lake

sometimes "hidden" in a light layer of fog. If you try to enjoy the view by rowing a boat in the lake, you might be attracted to stay there forever. However, visitors to the West Lake will not only appreciate its beauty, but they will also be fascinated by its rich culture.

The West Lake is famous for its top 10 attractions, including the dams, the moonlight, the fish, the singing birds, the reflection of the moon, the sunsets, and the bell. The decision to build one of the dams was made by Su Dongpo. Later, to pay respect for his effort, the dam was named after him, called Su Di (Su is his surname and Di means dam). In the early mornings in spring, the West Lake appears to come to life with birds singing, it is said that the scenery is especially unique. In addition to Su Di, there is also a Bai Di. Bai Di is named after the official and poet, Bai Juyi (772 – 846), who governed Hangzhou for three years. Under his management, he improved the water irrigation system, and constructed a dam to increase the amount of water held in the lake.

Tai Hu is also a famous lake in China and is the country's third largest fresh water lake. There is a story on how Tai Hu was formed. It was said that in the old times, there was a city near the lake. The mayor of the city was selfish and greedy, so he got involved in corruption and did many things to harm the citizens. One day, the mayor killed the husband of the Jellyfish Empress (a Taoist goddess, also known as Shuimu Niangniang). The Jellyfish Empress was very angry, so she took two buckets of water from the sea, intending to flood the city. When the Goddess of Mercy (also known as Guanyin) found out about this, she was deeply worried and came up with an idea. She turned herself into an old lady and approached the Jellyfish Empress, saying that she was very thirsty and needed some water. The Empress agreed to help, so the old lady took the bucket and drank all the water in it. The Jellyfish Empress then realised the old lady was no ordinary person, so she tried her best to take the other bucket back, and in the process accidentally poured the water all over the city. The city ended up like an ocean, and Tai Hu was formed. Since one bucket of water had been drunk by the Goddess of Mercy, the outskirts of the city were saved. Even these days, some fishermen claim that they can still find bricks and other bits and pieces from the old times.

Tai Hu has a coastline of 400 kilometres and covers over 300 hectares. The enormous Tai Hu has more than 60 small islands, which are like pearls scattered on the lake. Among the islands, there are large ones that provide shelter for people; there are also small ones that are almost at sea-level, that serve to divide the lake into a number of small districts. As a result, a unique scene is formed, where there are mountains after mountains in some sections, and lakes inside lakes in others. Fan Zhongyan (989 – 1052), a poet from the Northern Song Dynasty (960 – 1127), vividly described the various facets of the lake's beauty. "When it's active, there are waves, making the islands seem as though they are shaking in the lake. On the other hand, when it's silent, the water will be able to show reflections clearly, as the surface of the water is calm."

Except for its views, Tai Hu is also famous for its seafood. It is at the intersection of the Jiangsu and Zhejiang Provinces, where the weather is fine for most of the time, so lots of fish and shrimps are produced. Anchovies, white shrimps and a kind of mullet are the three best products. They are known as "the Three Treasures of Tai Hu". The spring season is the reproduction period, so no one is allowed to catch any fish. The harvesting starts in May, with mid-May being the peak period for fishing.

6 The Great Wall

Most of you have probably heard of the Great Wall in China. It used to be believed that two man made objects could be identified from space with the naked eyes were the dam in Rotterdam and the Great Wall in China. While this story is untrue it still captures the sheer size of the Great Wall.

The First Emperor of Qin Dynasty (259 BC – 210 BC), was looking for eternal peace after defeating the Huns (also known as Xiongnu), a tribe to the north of his kingdom. Therefore he ordered the Great Wall to be built. To complement such a majestic plan, all soldiers and most men in the country were recruited to work on it, and they worked day and night in extremely cold weather. The price to pay for such a project was massive, and many lives were lost in the process. Nevertheless, it successfully resisted any invasion of the northern tribes. The Wall also demonstrated architectural skills of ancient China. In fact, history books suggested that the Great Wall was not built in times when China was weak; to the contrary, it was built when China was strong, when it was under the rule of the First Emperor of Qin Dynasty and the Emperor Wudi of Han Dynasty (156 BC – 87 BC). Therefore we can conclude that the Great Wall was actually a warning to the northern tribes to stop invading across the border, so that everyone could live peacefully.

The Great Wall

The section of the Great Wall which is most visited is in Beijing, the capital of China. However, the full Great Wall stretches over a number of provinces, from Gansu in the west to Liaoning in the east. The construction started in the 7th or 8th century BC, while the Wall that exists today is mostly the result of some renovations done in the Ming Dynasty (1369 – 1644). To protect the borders, in the 200 odd years of the Ming Dynasty, maintenance and renovation works of a larger scale were performed around 18 times.

A lot of military passes had been established at strategic locations, like the Juyong Pass, the Jiayu Pass and the Shanhai Pass. Of these passes, the most important one was the Shanhai Pass, hence its nickname "the No.1 Pass". It was built under the leadership of Xu Da, the great general who was one of the most glorious warriors of the Ming Dynasty. It is located at a position where the mountain meets the sea, which is a strategically viable spot to defend against attacks from both the land and the sea. The wall of this pass is 14 metres tall, with signal stations all over it, making it a very solid military defence system.

7 The Forbidden City

Beijing is not only the current capital of modern China, but it has also been a popular capital city in the past. Beijing was the capital in the Yuan Dynasty (1271 – 1368), the Ming Dynasty (1369 – 1644) and the Qing Dynasty (1644 – 1911). Because of this, it has left us a legacy of various ancient architectural sites, in addition to the section of the Great Wall, which has fascinated tourists from all over the world.

One of them is the Forbidden City. It is at the heart of Beijing, and serves as the palace in both the Ming and Qing Dynasties. The construction of the palace started in 1406, and it took 14 years to complete. In the last 500 years, 24 emperors have lived in it. In the past, the palace was a place of restricted access, with all sorts of security measures taken to guard against outsiders, so it was called the Forbidden City. In 1925, it was named Gugong (meaning "former palace" if translated directly). It occupies an area of 720,000 square metres, which came second out of the 6 largest palaces of the world. It is also the most well-preserved ancient palaces of such scale, and it is the largest architectural structure made of wood. In addition, it is the largest museum in China, with over 100,000 exhibits.

Legends have it that there were 9,999 rooms in the Forbidden

The Forbidden City

City. As the emperor was regarded as the son of the Heavenly God, his palace must not have more rooms than the palace in Heaven (which was believed to have 10,000 rooms). Another tale is that in Chinese the pronunciation of "9" is the same as the word meaning "a long time", so having 9,999 rooms was a blessing that the empire would last forever. The Forbidden City can be divided into two parts, the external and the internal. The external part is where ceremonies were held and where the emperor met his officials; the internal part is the "bedroom palace", which included the office where the emperor worked, and where the queen and other concubines lived.

Being the residence of the emperor, the Forbidden City must be the most illustrious. As a result, the building materials, its colour and its height were all strictly fixed. No one could build his home similar to the emperor's palace. For example, traditionally, yellow represented the centre. Therefore, yellow was the main colour for the emperor's personal belongings, yellow tiles feature all through the Forbidden City, and yellow is a prominent theme colour throughout the palace. The Forbidden City used to be a mythical place because of the tight security, but now it is open to all tourists so that everyone can appreciate ancient China architecture.

8 The Ming Tombs

Another frequently-visited ancient architectural relic is the place where 13 emperors from the Ming Dynasty (1369—1644) were buried — the Ming Tombs. It was no easy task to pick a good site for the emperors' burial ground. First, Fengshui had to be taken into consideration, and then there was the problem of taboo. The Ming Tombs were surrounded by mountains in the east, west and north. In the south, there were two mountains too, which were just like a dragon and a tiger guarding the site. The construction work on the tombs started in 1409, and was completed over 230 years later, in 1644. It is 40 square kilometres, which is about 5,500 football fields put together.

The Ming Tombs are surrounded by a wall and there are 10 barriers dividing the enclosed area. There is a path 7 kilometres long along the central axis of the tombs, which runs from north to south. The Dragon Phoenix Gate (also known as the Longfeng Men) is also located along the path. People think that a gate in front of a tomb signifies the separation of the living world from that of the dead. Once you pass through the gate, it means that you have entered the world of the dead. Although the 13 Ming Tombs are different sizes, their designs are more or less the same. Generally, if the tomb was built before the emperor passed away, it would be of a larger scale and more luxurious.

The Ming Tombs above the ground are magnificent, but they are only decorations. The real architectural work is the palace under the ground. Recently, the tomb of the 13th emperor of the Ming Dynasty, Ding Ling, was found and is now set aside as an underground museum for visitors. The tomb palace of the emperor looks very similar to the palace he lived in when he was alive. It occupies an area of 1,195 square metres. There are 7 sets of big doors in the palace, each weighs a hefty 4 tonnes. The palace is formed by 5 halls, and the coffin of the emperor and the two queens were placed in the rear hall. Over 3,000 items were found interred with the dead, including the crowns of the emperor and the queens, the emperor's clothing, jewellery, money and clothes. All of these are now exhibited.

The Ming Tombs

9 The Capital of the Ten Dynasties — Xi'an

In modern times, Xi'an is the political, economic and cultural centre of Shaanxi Province. In the past, it was even more famous. Because it was named the capital city for many dynasties, Xi'an is considered the premier capital city on the entire list of China's ancient capital cities.

Xi'an is geographically in the centre of Shaanxi Province and is surrounded by mountains on all sides, so it is easy to defend and difficult to attack. That could be a reason why many empires chose Xi'an as their capital city. In the 1,000 years or so since the Western Zhou Dynasty (1066 BC – 771 BC), 10 dynasties chose Xi'an as their capital. During the Western Han Dynasty (206 BC – 23 AD) and Tang Dynasty (618 – 907), the capital was known as Chang'an instead of Xi'an. After the Tang Dynasty, it ceased being the capital and its name changed a few times. Eventually, during the Ming Dynasty (1369 – 1644) it was called Xi'an, and that name has been maintained till now.

During the Tang Dynasty, Chang'an was built to precise calculations and with careful planning. The city was mainly divided into three parts, namely Gong Cheng, Huang Cheng and Waikuo Cheng. The Gong Cheng was where the emperor worked, and also where the emperor and his concubines lived. The Huang Cheng was where the government officials worked, while the Waikuo Cheng was where the officials and other citizens lived. It was also the business area of the city.

During the Tang Dynasty, China was an extremely strong country and many neighbouring countries and tribes tried to establish diplomatic relations with China by sending diplomats to Chang'an. Visitors and delegations came from Asia, Europe and even Africa. Over 10,000 foreigners lived permanently in the city at that time and they included merchants, students, and religious followers. It was like a big metropolitan city, enjoying the fusion of music, dance and costumes from different countries and absorbing cultures from different nations.

Being the capital for 10 different dynasties, there are a lot of monuments, cultural and historical relics left in Xi'an, and there are many places of historic interest. Symbolic spots like the Old City Wall, the Big Wild Goose Pagoda, the Small Wild Goose Pagoda, Forest of Stone Steles Museum and of course, the Qin Terracotta Warriors, are all very popular tourist sites. Xi'an made use of this advantage and was developed a thriving tourism industry, bringing major economic development to the city.

One of the top eight sites

The Pagoda

in Xi'an is "the Pagoda and the Morning Bell". The Pagoda is the Small Wild Goose Pagoda, and it houses a big bell weighing over 10,000 kilograms. The Small Wild Goose Pagoda is not tall, but the layout of its floors is very intricate. There is an interesting legend about this pagoda. It was said that in the Ming Dynasty, the pagoda broke into two during a huge earthquake, and 34 years later, the two pieces simply joined into one during another huge earthquake. Therefore it was given the nickname Shen He Pagoda ("Shen He" can be directly translated as "amazingly combined").

10 | The Qin Terracotta Warriors

The Qin Terracotta Warriors were accidentally discovered in the spring of 1974, at the Xiyang Village of Lintong County, 35 kilometres east of Xi'an, by a few farmers who were looking for underground water sources. At that time, they were digging and suddenly a huge hole appeared. They dug deeper and gradually found bricks and some of the Terracotta Warriors. This attracted a great deal of interest but no one did anything about it at first. The farmers just took them to the fields and used as scarecrows.

A senior government official heard about this, and suspected that it might be some sort of historical treasure, so he reported the discovery to the Cultural Bureau. Archaeologists were alerted and eventually, the Terracotta Warriors, which had been buried underground for over 2,200 years, came into contact with the modern world. The discovery caused quite a stir in the world, and was called "the Eighth Wonder of the World". Ever since a museum was built in 1983, tourists come over from everywhere to see the site. UNESCO also added the Qin Terracotta Warriors to the World Heritage list in December 1987.

The Terracotta Warriors site is a unique, yet very organised underground construction. Within an area of 20,780 square metres, there were more than 7,000 Terracotta Warriors, each of a similar

The Qin Terracotta Warriors

size to real people, lined up in patterns within three big cavities. Everything that may be needed in wartime back then was there: chariots, bows, arrows, swords, halberds, poleaxes, and so on. Although they have suffered from erosion, they are still sharp and ready for use, and the Terracotta Warriors themselves are poised for immediate combat. The Qin Terracotta Warriors have always amazed visitors, and Jacques Chirac, the former president of France, once said that if one had not visited the Qin Terracotta Warriors, then he had not really visited China.

In the ancient times, it is essential to treat corpses with great respect. There was even a time when living humans were buried alive, together with the great leader of a tribe who had passed away. This practice gradually disappeared when living human beings were replaced by Terracotta soldiers. The Qin Terracotta Warriors are a great example of such a practice, but they also reflect how high the standard of sculpting was at that time. This also goes a long way to explain why the First Emperor of Qin Dynasty (259 BC – 210 BC) invested so many resources in producing such an army near his own tomb — its principal purpose would be to protect him after his death and to give him an army in the other world to scare off his enemies.

Chapter 4
Food and Sports

1 The Wide Variety of Chinese Cuisine

In the final years of the Southern Song Dynasty (1127 – 1279), Mongolian armies were invading the country constantly. The Song army was defeated and the emperor and his officials fled to the south, to reach the New Territories in Hong Kong. The citizens there were surprised to hear about the emperor's arrival, and they brought out their best food to welcome him. Since everything was done in a hurry, they did not have time to prepare the food well, so they simply put everything into big basins and served it to the emperor. To their surprise, the emperor and his officials were full of praise for the food, and the citizens then named the dish Pencai ("food in basin" if translated directly). This is how this delicious dish from the villages in Hong Kong has risen to fame as a cuisine.

In recent years, it has become a fashionable cuisine in Hong Kong. Restaurants and even fast food chains produce different kinds of Pencai to attract customers. In addition to the traditional one, there are seafood, vegetarian, western style, or single portion Pencai. In these variations, the range of ingredients used is increased. This trend has meant that this traditional village dish is now a popular dish in urban Hong Kong.

Pencai also has special cultural meanings, because it reflects harmony and equality. In the past, whenever there were celebrations, villagers would put a piece of red paper on their door, so that when others saw it, they would know that there would be Pencai served for visitors that night. During the meal, there are no rules to observe. Everyone can just chat and eat, no matter who they were. In this case, it

Pencai

definitely enhanced the relationship between people in the community. Traditionally a table of Pencai served 8 people. As it was usually a big event with many people, it operated in a way that whenever there were 8 people at a table, the food would be served for that table, so it was literally "first-come-first-served", no matter if the 8 people were rich or poor, or whether they were known to each other.

One of the other popular cuisine is Sichuan food. It is renowned for its spiciness and its most famous dish is Mapo Tofu (beancurd), which claims to provide a numb, hot, fresh, crisp and tender feeling at the same time. It was said that in the old times in Chengdu, there was a restaurant called Chen Xingsheng. The chief cook was the wife of the owner, who had a pockmarked face, so her nickname was Pockmarked Chen. The restaurant was located at a place where the oil merchants passed through when doing business and transporting oil, so it constantly attracted many merchants.

Of all kinds of food, tofu was the cheapest, so it was the most popular amongst the customers. However as time went on, people grew tired of the way they prepared the dish. It was always either fried or deep-fried. One day, a merchant handed some vegetable oil to Chen, asking her to cook him something different. Chen instantly came up with an idea, so she used chilli, fermented soybeans, thick broad-bean sauce, garlic, and some powdered herbs to cook a tofu dish which was spicy but smelled nice. The customer liked it so much after tasting it, so he called it Mapo Tofu. ("Mapo" can be translated to "pockmarked woman") This name became more and more popular as word spread really quickly in the old days.

Of course, there are other famous dishes in the Sichuan cuisine, such as Dry Roast Carp, Fish-flavoured Meat Slices, Gongbao Chicken Dices, Husband and Wife Lung Slices, Translucent Beef Slices, and Dandan Noodles. In terms of cooking methods, there are over 50 ways, including frying, deep-frying, baking, smoking, simmering, stewing, braising, boiling, and so on. The characteristics of Sichuan cuisine are its diverse rich tastes.

So what else is there other than this spicy style of food? There are eight main categories of Chinese cuisine based on their Province of origin: Shandong, Sichuan, Jiangsu, Zhejiang, Guangdong, Hunan, Fujian and Anhui. It is difficult to say which one of them is the best, because they each have their own distinct features. For example, Jiangsu cuisine emphasises the presentation of the dish, so it is delicately prepared and looks elegant. Guangdong cuisine focuses on the variety of cooking skills, so the dishes are always new and unique.

There are different types of banquets in different parts of China, each with its own speciality. For example, the Water Feast (also known as Shuixi) from the Luoyang Province consists of 24 dishes, including meat and vegetables, cold and hot dishes, sweet and salty dishes, as well as sour and spicy dishes, and it has over a thousand years' history. The name "Water Feast" has a double meaning: One is because all the dishes involve soup, and second is because dishes are served one after the other continuously, which is just like the continuous flow of water.

Apart from the Water Feast, there are also numerous feasts like Man-Han All Feast, All-Duck Feast, Cold Dishes Feast and Confucius Family (also known as Kongfu) Banquet. The dishes have been modified over time. But because they still taste good and continue to be so popular they have become a special aspect of Chinese food culture.

The magnificent cooking skills, the rich number of delicious dishes and the interesting stories behind the dishes all contribute to make Chinese cuisine an art where it satisfies people's vision, taste and smell. All kinds of Chinese cooking put a strong emphasis on three basic rules: the food must look good, smell good and taste good. It sounds simple, but there are a lot of skills involved. Usually, colourful ingredients like those in red, yellow, green and white are used in support of the main ingredient, so as to make the dishes look nice.

The Chinese use spring onion, ginger, garlic, wine, sesame oil, chilli and other spices, which add an attractive aroma to the food. Chefs also strive for a balance of the five tastes: sweet, sour, bitter, spicy and salty. As we all know, different food taste differently, therefore a good cook must be able to mix and match suitable ingredients in order to create a dish that can fulfil the three basic rules. Due to differences in climate, resources and customs, cooking and eating habit of different regions varies. This allows chefs to perform differently, so that numerous regional cuisines have been established, and a complicated yet brilliant food culture has emerged.

2 Table Manners and Dining in China

Traditionally, the Chinese place a lot of emphasis on "respect", so naturally the manners and customs involved in preparing a meal is an important part of China's food culture. The preparation varied from different dynasties, different social classes, and different situations; however, the important thing which remained unchanged was "respect".

The most sophisticated case of all would be the arrangements for the emperor's meal. When the emperor had a meal, he was always served by more than ten servants. As for the food, there was a clear set of rules from the utensils used to the style and number of dishes served. On an ordinary day, there would be two tables of dishes, a steamboat would be added in winter, including dim sums, rice and congee which amounted to three tables, and another small table of appetizers. As for the plates and bowls used, there would always be a dragon drawn on each of them marked with words saying "The emperor will live forever." But why make it so complicated, you may ask. The answer is simple: It is because for the emperor, eating is not just about filling his stomach, but also for showing that he is superior to the others.

A lot of old rules about appropriate behaviour at a meal times have been abolished, however, those that are related to banquets

The Simulation of an Emperor's Meal

have been kept. For a banquet, the host would normally invite guests by sending out invitations, and then welcoming them at the door on the day of the banquet. Guests must dress accordingly and they may bring gifts if they have a close enough relationship with the host.

Upon arrival, the guests must not just take a seat randomly; instead, they should wait for the host's arrangement. This particular point — the host arranging the seats — is one of the most important parts of the Chinese eating culture, because it shows the mutual respect between people. This not only happens in China, in fact, this is also true in many parts of the world. At the table, the best respected person or the eldest one would normally take the head seat, while relatives or the youngest ones would take the seats at the other end of the table. Nowadays when we attend a banquet, we still see that one or two tables are only for the host's families, usually nearest to the stage or platform. It would be considered rude for guests to sit there without asking the host.

Traditionally the Chinese place a high value on respecting the elderly. Apart from welcoming and arranging the seat order, during the meal, whenever a dish is served, people should wait for the most respected person to make the first move, or they can put some food from the dish into the bowl of that person, before actually starting to eat. If a person does not do so, he would be considered rude. One more thing guests would do is never finish everything on the plate, so as to avoid embarrassing the host by sending a wrong message that the host has not prepared enough food.

One thing that is common in Chinese eating cultures is that everyone sits together around a table, meaning, the host is sitting with the guests, and everyone shares the food communally. Since the Song Dynasty (960 – 1279), it was very common to have 8 or more persons at a table eating together. Nowadays, this format has become a characteristic of the Chinese eating culture.

The Chinese have always valued eating. Whenever it is a full month after a baby was born, or when there is a birthday, a marriage, or when it is New Year and other major festivals, a banquet will be organised, where the whole family sit together and celebrate. Also, when someone has passed away, the family would also organise a meal right after the funeral, as an act to show the gratefulness to those who have attended the funeral. One significant importance of a banquet is to provide an opportunity for people to stay together and share the happiness and sadness in life. Therefore on such an occasion, there is always a warm atmosphere, reflecting a harmonious relationship within the family and also the community.

One of the greatest differences between the Chinese food culture and Western food culture is that the Chinese use chopsticks while western people use forks and knives. Chopsticks were first used in the Shang Dynasty (16th century BC – 1066 BC), and before that, according to the archaeologists, ancient Chinese used a couple of tools made of bones of wild animals, which were shaped like a knife and a spoon. Chopsticks were called "Zhu" in the past, which sounds the same as another word which means "stop". People always preferred things to go smoothly rather than having interruptions, so later they called it "Kuai" (which sounds the same as "fast") instead. There is another taboo involving the use of chopsticks and that is, not to hit the bowls and plates with chopsticks. This is because only beggars do so. Moreover, this is an action to show dissatisfaction with the quality of the food or the speed in serving the food, so it is a rude act and should be avoided.

The chopsticks are flexible tools and can be used in various ways to enable a person to eat or handle food. If used well, they are just like an extension of one's own fingers. Chopsticks are always seen as something that brings good fortune to people, and they are also used in wedding celebrations. These days, chopsticks are considered highly appropriate wedding gifts.

3 | Wine Culture

There is a story about an orphaned teenager called Du Kang. Du was a shepherd and everyday he would bring a herd of sheep up the hills, taking some rice with him for food. When he was on the hills, he started to think about his parents, which made him really sad. Because of the sadness, he lost his appetite and threw his rice into the hole of a tree. Gradually, Du became thinner and thinner, which made his uncle think that he might be allergic to broomcorn rice. Therefore, he started to give him millet instead. Of course, he did not feel any better, so he did the same with the millet, again, throwing it into the hole with the broomcorn rice.

Not long afterwards, he smelled some aroma, coming from the hole in the tree. He then noticed that the hole was overflowing with liquid. Out of curiosity, he sipped a bit of the liquid, and it tasted nice. He wondered where the liquid had come from, and suspected that it came from a chemical reaction between the broomcorn rice and millet. When he returned to the village, he repeated what he did, and successfully created this drink which had a special aroma. His fellow villagers tasted it and were all full of praise.

As you probably have guessed it, that is how Du accidentally made the first wine in China. From then on, people simply used "Du Kang" to represent wine. Actually, China is the first country to produce wine, and historical records on wines can be found even on inscriptions on animal bones. Drinking culture is ancient and the literati gave a lot of "nicknames" to wine, like "Wang You" (forget troubles) and "Bei Zhong Wu" (something in the glass), all of which have appeared in various poems.

There are a few ways to name wine. One way is to name it by its origin, like Maotai and Shaoxing Jiu. Another way is to name it by its ingredients, like Wuliangye (liquid of the 5 grains) and Zhuye Qing (green bamboo leaves). Some wines are even named after famous historical persons, like Wenjun Jiu, Guifei Jiu and Taibai Jiu. Amongst all the great wines in China, Maotai is the most famous. It is a white wine, with a relatively high percentage of alcohol (53%). It is obviously strong but not dry; the wine is crystal clear and transparent and has a light taste. Maotai is often served in international banquets, hence it is also known as "the National Wine" and "the Wine for Guests" (also known as Libin Jiu).

There is story about how Maotai was introduced to the international scene. Rumour has it that at the Panama World Expo in 1915, the organising committee refused to let Maotai enter the exhibition due to its poor packaging. Luckily a representative from the Chinese team thought of a great idea — he intentionally dropped a bottle of Maotai on the floor. The bottle broke and the wine came out, suddenly the hall was filled with its aroma, which attracted a lot of the representatives. They tasted it and everyone was very impressed and in the end, Maotai was ranked among the world's best wines, alongside Scotch Whiskey and French Brandy.

In different festivals, people drink different wine, like drinking Xionghuang Jiu during the Dragon Boat Festival, Chrysanthemum Wine during the Double Ninth Festival and Tusu Jiu during the New Year. Nowadays, these habits have faded gradually, although

Chinese Wine

one thing has not changed — wine is still essential in festival celebrations and banquets. Some traditional customs are wine-related too. When a baby is a month old, parents have to organise a dinner gathering called Manyue Jiu (Full-month Wine). On the day of marriage, one of the procedures for a marriage includes the couple drinking a glass of wine each, with their arms locked together. After a funeral, there is also a meal to thank those attended the funeral, which also involves wine to wash away anything unpleasant.

In the old times, literati often gathered to appreciate poems, drink wine and have fun. There was a reason as to why so many of them liked wine. It was because through wine, they could express their feelings deep in their hearts; wine "enhanced" their happiness when they were happy, and "supported" them when they felt dreadful. Li Bai (701 – 762), one of the most distinguished poets, held many drinking sessions with friends when career opportunities did not come to him. He expressed his belief that life was short and chances for him to be successful during this short life were minimal. Whereas another famous person Ouyang Xiu (1007 –

1072), governor of Xu Zhou, often went with guests to a pavilion in the mountains for a drink. He could not drink much, so he called himself "the Drunken Man", and named the pavilion "the Drunken Man's Pavilion". He even wrote an essay about the pavilion, which was passed on till this day, because of its memorable lines.

Generally literati loved to walk around and visit mountains and lakes, enjoying the beauty of nature; the presence of wine would definitely enhance their enjoyment. If there is such a love of wine, were there lots of drunkards in China then? No, apparently not. There is a "rule" stating that, after drinking three glasses of wine a man must exert some self-discipline, and put down his glass.

4 | Tea Culture

There is a story about the beginnings of tea drinking. Over 5,000 years ago, there was a person called Shennong Shi, who had a transparent stomach so he could always observe his reactions to the digestion of the different foods he had eaten. To increase the variety of herbs people could take, he decided to investigate different herbs by tasting all the plants. One day, after he had eaten a leaf, he noticed that the leaf was travelling non-stop to the stomach as if it was examining something. A little later, all the dirty substances in his stomach were gone! He called it "Cha" (means "check" in English), and gave it to people when they were sick. Later on it became the present day Cha ("cha" is the nickname for "tea" in English), which is pronounced in the same way but is a different character in Chinese. Nowadays, tea is seen as a healthy drink, it helps to reduce tiredness and is also efficient in cooling people down. It can also help to prevent cancer, various eye diseases and aging, as well as cure skin diseases.

Similar to food, the criteria for deciding whether a tea is good or not are its colour, smell and taste. Some other details are also considered, like its place of origin, the kind of tree that produced the leaves, and who produced it. From this we can tell that it is not easy for a tea to be classified as a good tea. Biluochun is one of the most famous teas in China. Let us tell you how it became popular. It was said that one year, a lot of tea trees grew on the Biluo Mountain. Nobody knew where it came from, but everyone went to collect the tea leaves. On their way back, they noticed that everyone had the same aroma, which was a very pleasant smell. Then they realised that their body heat had warmed the tea leaves and caused the aroma to be released from the leaves. Later, an emperor in the Qing Dynasty (1644 – 1911), Kangxi (1662 – 1722), visited Suzhou and tried this tea, which he loved a lot and named it Biluochun. Apart from it, Longjing, Dahongpao, Tieguanyin and Maofeng are some other famous teas in China.

Chinese Tea

China is known as the home of tea, and tea is the "National Drink" of China. Whenever there is a guest, the host would always serve the guest with tea, otherwise he will be considered rude. Naturally, in China there are lots of written works on tea. The first book of such kind was *The Book of Tea* (also known as *Cha Jing*), written by Lu Yu (733 – 804), who is known as "the Saint of Tea".

Just like most other famous people, there is a story behind Lu Yu. In ancient times, there was a monk called Jigong living in a temple. One day, Jigong saw a group of wild geese gathering at the riverside, all of them flapping their wings. He went closer to see what happened out of curiosity, and when he got close enough, he saw a baby who had been dumped, being fed by the wild geese. The monk felt a sudden connection to the baby, so he took it with him on his way back, naming it Lu Yu. As he grew up, Jigong started to ask Lu to perform some easy tasks. He asked him to make tea as well as take care of cows. Since then, Lu's interest in tea started to grow. To know more about tea, he travelled everywhere, especially to places where tea leaves were grown, in order to collect data about tea leaves, and learn about how to prepare different teas, as well as techniques in making different teas. After some years of hard work, Lu wrote the first book of tea.

Nearly everything about tea can be found in *The Book of Tea*. There are chapters on harvesting and producing tea leaves, apparatus for cooking tea, the good and bad of different kinds of water for tea, habits and customs of drinking tea. It enriched the art and the cultivation of tea, significantly affecting the tea culture in China. "The art of tea" refers to the art of producing tea, making tea and tasting tea. Lu paid a lot of attention to the art of tea, providing very strict requirements for the way a tea is produced, the apparatus, the water and the temperature used in making the tea. In tasting tea, he gave opinions on the tea leaves from different parts of China and the water as well. His strict requirements in achieving the art of tea had a great impact on his followers.

Nowadays, various scholars claim that the moral values of people could be raised through the appreciation of the art of tea culture. Tea culture in China has had widespread impact, and the tea culture in Japan is largely influenced by the traditional customs from China, aiming at the mutual respect between people, and achieving a state of calm and peacefulness in the inner self.

The pace of living in the modern world is really fast. However during weekends and holidays, restaurants in Hong Kong and many other cities in China are always packed with people. They sit together, have a nice chat and enjoy the tea and dim sum in a very relaxed way. This activity not only gives people a chance to recharge themselves over the weekend, but also provides an occasion for families or friends to meet up and keep in touch from time to time.

5 | Martial Arts and Sports

Shaolin martial arts are held in high regard in the world of Chinese martial arts. Shaolin Temple is the birthplace of Shaolin martial arts and it is located on the Song Mountain in Henan Province. As early as in the Southern and Northern Dynasties (960 –1279), there were two monks from the Shaolin Temple who were extremely good at martial arts. They were called Huiguang and Seng Ti. It was said that when Huiguang was twelve, he could stand on a fence on one leg while playing with a shuttlecock with the other leg, keeping it in the air for over 500 consecutive kicks. Shaolin martial arts started to become famous at the early Tang Dynasty (618 – 907), when the emperor got help from the monks in fighting his enemies. Eventually, the emperor gave Shaolin Temple 40 hectares of land, and named one of the monks, Tanzong, as a general. Since then, the name Shaolin Temple's fame has spread everywhere.

In many films and martial arts novels, *Yijin Jing* is described as a book containing some martial arts training instructions, so those who get hold of it and practice the martial arts set out there will become the best fighters of his era. However in the real world, *Yijin Jing* is only a book showing some everyday exercises which everyone can do to stay healthy. Out of all the different moves, Shaolin Quan

Shaolin Martial Arts

(Shaolin punches) is the most respected. It is practical, efficient yet flexible. Apart from punches, Shaolin is also famous for its gun moves (fighting with a stick), which are considered the best among other subgroups of stick fighting in China.

Before learning martial arts, one will always learn about this sentence first: "Learn to respect before learning how to fight, learn about moral values before learning the moves." This is exactly what martial arts is about. Its existence is for self-defence and strengthening the body, but not to harm or hurt others. There are also rules in martial arts contests. Only certain parts of the body can be hit, which are the parts that are not fatal if hurt, like the mouth, knees, and cheeks. However the important parts of the body like the ribs, the two sides of the head and neck cannot be hit. If a person attacks his opponent on these areas, not only will he lose his match, but others will look down on him forever for his lack of respect. It is important that the contestants greet each other face to face before the contest, and they are not allowed to attack from the back, because this is seen as cowardly.

After talking about martial arts, let us look at some sports activities. In the past, there was an activity called "Cuju". It means kicking a ball literally, which seems to be a game that is very similar to modern soccer. When Liu Bang (256 BC – 195 BC) established the Western Han Dynasty (206 BC – 23 AD), he brought his parents over to the palace to live with him. However he noticed that his father was unhappy in the palace, so he sent his men to try to find out why. In the end he discovered that his father missed the old times when he played Cuju with his friends. Therefore the emperor built a new city in resemblance to the old town the family used to live in, and then invited the old friends and neighbours to move in so that there would be enough players to play the game with his father. In the Tang Dynasty (618 – 907), this activity became ever so popular among the public, even women and children started playing it.

There was another activity which was rather popular, which started from the Song Dynasty (960 – 1279). It was called "Chuiwan". It is an activity that is very similar to the game of golf nowadays. The game was developed from the Tang Dynasty. At that time, there was a game where people used a stick to strike a ball. In the Yuan Dynasty (1271 – 1368), there was even a book about the game called *Wan Jing*. According to the book, the game was played on a piece of land. On the land, some holes would be dug and a flag would be put right next to it. The game could be played in groups or individually, and there were rules in preventing others interfering with the person striking the ball, preventing anyone to move the ball randomly, and preventing the change of the striking stick during the match. The game was very popular until the Qing Dynasty (1644 – 1911), when some other sports activities became popular. It is believed that Chuiwan might have been introduced to the Europeans by the Mongolians in the 13th century, and it eventually evolved into the game of golf.

Some traditional sports in China came from military practices, like Cuju, polo and weight-lifting. In the army, the game Cuju was played to liven up soldiers and to raise their spirits. The Chinese have always emphasised moral values and a harmonious relationship between people, so even in sports games, they were seldom too aggressive.

Chapter 5
Arts and Crafts

1 Chinese Pottery and Porcelain

Yixing County of Jiangsu Province produces pottery extensively, and has long been known as the capital of pottery. The "Five Golden Flowers" (five kinds of ceramics), namely zisha, qingtao, juntao, caitao and jingtao are all extremely famous. Since the Northern Song Dynasty (960 – 1127), people liked to use zisha (purple clay) teapot to make tea, because they could enjoy the colour, smell and taste of tea better with it. There was a story around the southern areas, saying that there was once a builder who had forgotten about his teapot while working, and he accidentally placed it in the ceiling. A few years later, he was asked to fix the house, and he discovered that the tea in the teapot was still fresh. The builder exclaimed, "The purple clay teapot is the real deal. The tea kept in it just won't turn bad!" Purple clay teapots are usually delicate pieces of art themselves, with traditional Chinese drawings, calligraphy and seal cuttings on them, which amaze people and make it impossible for one not to own at least one of them.

Since clay can be moulded easily, people have created all kinds of ceramics using their imagination. The most famous example is the Qin Terracotta Warriors. Each Warrior has a different facial expression, but they appear to be commanding nonetheless, which is really amazing. As people learnt the skills of producing ceramics, they tried to produce all kinds of tools that could be used in daily lives in order to raise their living standards, like water pipes, storage containers, cooking utensils, and bricks. Caitao (coloured ceramics) is a special aspect of the Chinese pottery and porcelain culture. Coloured ceramics are a moulded ceramic piece painted with other coloured substances, and then the colour is fixed by heating. Tang Sancai, a fusion of the art of producing sculptures and the art of producing ceramics, is the most popular type of coloured ceramics,

Tang Sancai

and is famous for its excellent colouring and numerous styles.

Chinese porcelains have a long history and they are one of the greatest achievements of Chinese art culture. They attract people by their colour and beauty. During the Qing Dynasty (1644 – 1911), there was a foreigner called Badeng, who was in China supposedly to preach Christianity, when in fact he was trying to collect famous porcelain pieces of the past and learn the technique in producing these items. One day, he arrived at a big temple, and he soon fixed his eyes on the porcelain of the Goddess of Mercy (also known as Guanyin). Badeng thought to himself, "It would be great if I could take this delicately produced, brilliantly coloured porcelain away!" So he found the monk in the temple and proposed to buy it. However, the monk told him that it was not for sale. Badeng was not satisfied with the answer, so he waited for a chance, and at one moment when the monk was not looking, he took the porcelain away and left the temple.

The monk was very worried when he discovered that the Goddess of Mercy was gone. At that time, Zhou Danquan, an expert in imitating ancient porcelain, visited the temple. After knowing what had happened, he comforted the monk and told him he could get it back for him. A few days later, Zhou visited the church in which Badeng was working. He told him that he had a porcelain Goddess of Mercy and asked if Badeng was interested in buying it. Badeng was very surprised because the porcelain figure looked exactly the same as the one he had stolen from the temple. Zhou continued, "There is only one genuine piece, all the others are imitations." After that, he walked away and pretended not to be looking. Badeng took the chance and swapped his stolen one for Zhou's figure. Of course, that meant he actually swapped the real one for the fake.

It was said that the Goddess of Mercy that was stolen by Badeng was made in Jingde Town, nicknamed as "the Capital of Porcelain", the famous base for the production of porcelain. Back in the Northern Song Dynasty (960 – 1127), which was more than a thousand years ago, it was originally called Changnan Town. During the Jingde years (Jingde is the title of the emperor in reign), the emperor ordered the town to make pottery items that were to be used by the emperor; at the bottom of each pottery, the words "Made in Jingde Years" were inscribed. From then on, the potteries from Changnan Town became very famous, and later, people simply called the area Jingde Town instead of its original name.

The word "china" means pottery. Pottery from China were traded all over Europe and Asia, therefore "China" became the name of the country that produced such high quality products, and this was how china obtained its name. Pottery from China are popular not only because they stick to the traditional techniques strictly, but also because there are constant advances in techniques and colourings, and new elements are introduced in shaping too. These innovative ideas have enabled the traditional techniques to keep up with the pace of the modern times, and the pottery items were useful in daily life, thus giving people opportunities to appreciate and enjoy its beauty and artistry.

2 Precious Stones of China

There are quite a few popular legends related to jade. There was once a man in the country of Chu by the name of Bian He. One day, while he was going up to the mountains to collect some wood, he saw a phoenix resting on a stone. Suddenly he remembered an old saying, "Phoenix only rests on treasures", and therefore he firmly believed that the stone on which the phoenix rested must be a rare gem. He then decided to give it to the king. King Li called on a specialist in gemstones to have a look at that stone, but the specialist told him that it was only an ordinary stone. He was so angry that he decided to cut Bian's left leg off to punish him for trying to deceive him. King Li died not long after this, and a man named Wu became the new king. Bian again took the stone with him and went to see the new king. Once again he handed over the stone which he believed was a gem. King Wu consulted another specialist on gemstones and again, the specialist reported that it was just an ordinary stone. He was outraged and he ordered to have Bian's right leg cut off for trying to trick him.

Some time later, Wu passed away and Wen became the new king. Bian had lost both legs so he could not go to see the king to offer the gemstone. He was so sad about it that he cried for three whole days, and when his tears dried up eventually blood came out instead of tears. This piece of news spread over the city instantly, and King Wen heard of it too. He sent his men to bring him and his gemstone into the palace, then he asked the specialist to perform a detailed check and to cut it open carefully. Soon, the good news came: The specialist came running to the king to tell him that it was a very rare piece of jade! The king was very touched by his persistence and loyalty, so he named it "Bian He's Jade".

From the fact that a piece of jade generated such interesting legends, we can see how valuable jade is to the Chinese people. A popular belief amongst the Chinese is that jade can repel evil things and attract happiness, so we can find that many jade figures are related to good luck, longevity, and happiness. Children are told to carry a piece of jade with them so that they will be blessed. Another popular idea related to jade is that people believed that putting a jade cicada into the mouth of the deceased would give them a new life, because although the life of a cicada is short, it lives longer as a caterpillar and would eventually turn into a cicada, which is just like having a new life. Here we can see that in jade, people always look for happiness and that is priceless, hence there is a

Jade

saying that gold is valuable, but jade is priceless.

In China, there are seals in various forms, but the most precious one must be the jade seal used by the emperors in all dynasties. It is the symbol of the highest power, just like the crown in the West. Seals used to be called "Xi", until the Qin Dynasty (221 BC – 206 BC) when the First Emperor decided that the word "Xi" would be solely used by the emperor. Other seals could only be called "Yin". Later on, Wu Zetian (624 – 705) became the female emperor and she thought that "Xi" sounded similar to the word for death (which is "Si"), so she changed it to "Bao" (meaning "treasure"), and this name has remained in use since then.

Many materials can be used to make a seal, like jade, gold, silver, stone, bone, agate, and amber. On seals, various fonts can be seen. These seals are good examples of the unique Chinese art of calligraphy and carvings combined together. There were strict restrictions on the content of seals of the emperor and the officials, whereas it was free for ordinary citizens to decide what to carve on seals. Some would have words carved on them, while others would have pictures of animals instead. Nowadays, youngsters prefer to add more personal touch and style to their seals, like using their favourite cartoon characters or even their own images. It is true that these days, a personal signature has taken over the use of a seal to represent a person for practical purposes. However, from the artistic perspective, seals exist for their irreplaceable beauty. A drawing or a writing is perceived to look much better with a stamped seal of classic design at its corner.

3 | Needlework and Paper-cuts

In the past, Chinese women had to learn weaving, sewing and needlework. Needlework is the skill of making use of needles and coloured threads to create patterns on textile fabrics. Gradually it became a standard practice for women: the more skilful they were, the more highly they were regarded. Women could even use it to express their feelings towards the person they loved by embroidering certain flowers on a purse and giving it to that person. Needlework is one of the greatest traditional crafts in China; it has a history of about 3,000 years. There are different characteristics of needlework from different regions of China, of which Su, Xiang, Yue and Shu are known as the four best regions in embroidering. Su's embroidery is also called the Pearl of the East because it is colourful and the work is always delicate. The most famous piece of Su's embroidery is the "Cat". It is a two-sided work, so you can see the image of a cat on both sides of the artwork. Craftsmen (or craftswomen, for that matter) use threads that are half as thick as hair, and some that are even thinner, to stitch the cat. They even manage to hide thread knots so the threads end perfectly. The highlight of the work is the eyes of the cat, where craftsmen used more than 20 different coloured threads to make the eyes look bright and lively. Since the Ming Dynasty (1369 – 1644), craftsmen merged painting and needlework, creating needlework by embroidering scenes of mountains and lakes, and winning praise for "making paintings with needles".

Su's Embroidery

Apart from the four best regions in embroidering, there are many other special types of needlework in China, like Fa Xiu, which uses human hair as threads to create works with colours that will never fade. Many traditional skills have been forgotten nowadays, but needlework is not one of them. This is because people are creative and they always inject new elements into traditional needlework, for example, some modern needlework has partially absorbed the elements of the Western arts, thus a new style is established. This sort of freshness has certainly helped to maintain the status of traditional needlework.

Another popular art in China is paper-cutting. This art is deeply related to seasonal changes. For example, during the Mid-Autumn Festival, people would put up a paper-cut of Chang'e, a rabbit or a moon, because of a legend in which a lady called Chang'e and a rabbit were believed to live on the moon. During the Dragon Boat Festival, many people in the northern part of China would display paper-cuts of a calabash on the front door. Let us tell you the story behind it. It was said that Lü Dongbin (796 – ?), one of the Eight Fairies, pretended to be an oil-seller in a village. He used an honesty system that gave people the freedom to take and pay without him checking the quantities and money. Most people took more than what they paid for. There was a boy who did the same, but when he returned home, his mother scolded him and asked him to return the extra oil. The boy followed his mother's advice and did just that, he also apologised to the oil-seller for doing so. Lü was touched by him, so he told the boy that on the first day of May, there would be a flood. He told the boy to hang a calabash on the front door to avoid being drowned. The boy took Lü's advice and told his friends about this. On that day, floods really happened. Those who had a calabash hanging on their front door were not harmed at all, where many others were drowned. From then on, people would put up a calabash on the front door on the first day of May. Later, paper-cuts of a calabash replaced the real calabash.

Paper-cut is more than merely cutting paper. To make a good paper-cut, firstly the mind of the person must be clear, so that he

Paper-cut

would be able to concentrate. Secondly, he has to be calm. Thirdly he has to sit properly so that he can read the pattern properly. Next, he has to think carefully about where to start and plan how to create the pattern. Finally he has to be really careful, paying attention to the finest details so that a perfect work can be created. People like to express their wishes through paper-cutting. Usually, animals or flowers are used to represent blessings. Sometimes, words are also used, which express the wishes more directly. For example, the word "Xi" (made up of "Double Happiness" together) is used to congratulate a newly-married couple, "Fu" for good fortune in life, "Lu" for a smooth career and "Shou" for long life. These artworks effectively reflect the wisdom and imagination of people in the past.

4 | The Four Treasures of a Study

Pens, paper, ink and ink stones are known as the four treasures of a study. In ancient China, these four treasures were hugely important to all those who wrote and created. There are many stories about the Chinese literati and the four treasures. One of them is about the great poet Li Bai (701 – 762). It was said that when Li was young, he once dreamed of a beautiful flower growing from the tip of the pen that he was using. Since then, he had a great talent in writing poems and he ended up writing many great poems, winning the nickname "the Immortal Poet". Till this day, in Chinese we use the idiom Miaobi Shenghua (which can be directly translated as "a brilliant pen that bears flowers") to describe someone who is talented in writing literary works.

Pens are first among the four treasures. Here, the pen refers to the Chinese writing brush, which is a unique invention. The brush Hubi from Huzhou of Zhejiang Province is known as the king of brushes for its pointed end, which gives a nice end

The Four Treasures

to each stroke. It has been widely used since the Yuan Dynasty (1271 – 1368). As we all know, China is the first country to use paper and it was a Chinese who invented paper to write on. Xuan city from Anhui Province produces Xuan paper which is renowned for its durability — it is rarely eaten by ants or other organisms and it does not turn yellow for a very long time.

The literati were good at using ink for both calligraphy and drawings. Ink from the Anhui Province is known as the king of inks, this is because the ink will not fade, even if water is poured onto the page. Ink stones are used to ground ink. Ink stones from the Guangdong Province are most famous for their quality and colour of the material, as well as their classical and elegant appearance. These four treasures are of practical use but they are also collector's items. Some people collect these beautiful and delicate artworks, and the really good ones can cost a fortune.

The four treasures are not only the companions of literati, but they are also regarded as treasures within Chinese cultural arts. Their presence allows the Chinese to have their unique calligraphy and drawings. Wang Xizhi (303 – 361), who lived in the Eastern Jin Dynasty (317 – 420), is the most famous calligrapher in China. He was so good at calligraphy that people call him "the Saint of Calligraphy". It was said that Wang loved geese a lot. He thought that by paying attention to the movement of geese, he could calm himself down, as well as find inspiration for correctly holding and using the brush. He hoped he could work with the brush like the neck of a goose, where he could move his wrist freely in any directions, and use the brush with power concentrated at the end of the pen, just like the feet of a goose splashing the water.

Besides getting inspiration from the movements of geese, Wang also practiced a lot. One day his servant tried to serve him

Lanting Xu by Wang Xizhi

with bread and vinegar for dinner but couldn't get any response, so he asked Wang's wife for help. She came over to ask him to eat before he continued practicing, only to see that he was dipping the bread in the black ink and then putting them in his mouth. Then he complained that the taste was bad and he spat out the food, where upon she laughed and told him what he had just done.

The characteristic of Wang's calligraphy is that it looks neat and natural, with just the right level of strength applied in writing. His work Lanting Xu is a classic. It was written after he had a few glasses of wine. He was in the mood to write at that time, and he wrote the whole passage in one go; the characters were clear and beautiful, and they were written with just the right amount of power. Even if there were repeated characters, they looked a little different: Some were rigid and neat, some were free like fluid. People regard it as an example of top class calligraphy. Unfortunately that the authentic version was buried together with the Emperor Taizong in the Tang Dynasty (618 – 907), so any versions we now see are imitations.

5 | Chinese Paintings

Chinese paintings can be divided into water-ink paintings and coloured-ink paintings. In water-ink paintings the main element of the painting is ink, which is a greyish black colour. Adding different amounts of water to ink will produce different effects, like dry, wet, dark, light, and solid. These effects are used in place of colours, so no matter whether it is the skin of an old tree, a hard stone, or the soft petal of a flower, with the use of different effects of ink and the various pen techniques, it can be drawn accurately. On the other hand, coloured-ink paintings, obviously, use different colours and black ink. Ancient painters used to draw the outline first with ink and then fill in the colours. Later on, it was influenced by Western paintings, where painters often paint with colours and ink mixed together.

Chinese paintings place a lot of stress on combining penmanship, poetry and drawing. So there is an emphasis on the possibility of relating a painting to a poem, where the story of the poem is shown in the painting. For example, in the painting by Ma Yuan (1190 – 1255) in the Southern Song Dynasty (1127 – 1279), there is only a small boat, a person concentrated on fishing, a few layers of waves near the boat and nothing more in the surroundings. This reminded people of the famous poem Jiang Xue by Liu Zongyuan (773 –

Fishing Alone on an Iced River by Ma Yuan

819), which is about an old man fishing alone on a cold winter's day when the river is covered with snow.

A poem and a painting belong to two different categories in art, but Chinese painters manage to link them up, creating the imagination of "a painting within a poem" and "a poem within a painting". Some may say that the painting *Fishing Alone on an Iced River* is too simple. However, the blank spots give people unlimited imagination. Why is there only one person in the river? Why are there no birds in the sky? Is that person enjoying himself or is he lonely? Leaving some room for imagination is something that is very important in Chinese traditional paintings. Leaving it blank does not mean there is nothing there, it could be some fog, or some clouds, or it could also be water in the river. The better artistic effect is created by stretching the imagination of readers.

This painting is considered one of the best not only because of its setting and its use of ink effects, but also the presence of the painter's feelings in it. In other words, in addition to paying attention to the details of the objects drawn, the painter must also show the inner beauty of the objects, so as to show what he is thinking at that moment. In this painting, the inner feeling of the painter — loneliness — is perfectly shown, which is why it is considered one of the best.

Another famous Chinese painter is Qi Baishi (1864 – 1957), also known as "White Stone Old Man". He was very interested in painting from when he was very young, but because of the poor financial condition of his family, Qi had to frequently help out his family by sharing tasks like chopping wood, growing vegetables, shepherding the animals and fishing. He acquired a lot of techniques from the ancient painters; and he drew the people, farming tools, animals, plants and other common scenes around him in the village. Because of that, he was given the nickname "Artist of the People". For example, one of his famous works was the drawing *Picking One's Ear*. In the drawing, there was an old man sitting on a bamboo chair picking his ear, and conveyed that moment of pleasure. From this, we can see his sense of humour.

Qi was best at painting shrimps. Through the use of different shades of black ink, he made the shrimps look extremely lively. Moreover, when he was painting organisms in water like shrimps, crabs, tadpoles, and fish, he would paint them in a way that they were all swimming in the same direction. This would allow the audience to feel the liveliness that came from the group moving towards a direction together. Besides the rich content of nature, his paintings were also full of wisdom. One good example was the painting of two chicks fighting for a worm. He did not name the painting *Fighting Pair* or something along that, but named it *Getting Along Well Later On* instead, so it is like referring to kids fighting for over a toy or having some minor argument, where they will all get along well eventually after the fight or the argument is over.

Getting Along Well Later On by Qi Baishi

Qi was famous for having his own style in paintings. So how did he do it? Once, when he was asked about his painting abilities, he said that although he learned from others, he did not just imitate them. What he learned is the use of pen and colour but not the outcome of it. He thought out of the box, where he created his own style by putting lively artistic features of people into traditional Chinese paintings.

6 | Architectural Beauty

"Shiku" is the abbreviation for Shiku temple, which refers to Buddhist temples that are built on cliffs and rocks. Shiku first appeared in India, and are usually formed by a number of caves located just next to each other. Mogao Ku (also known as the Thousand Buddhas Cave located at the Mingsha Mountain at the south-east of Dunhuang in Gansu Province), Yungang Shiku (located at Datong in the Shanxi Province), Longmen Shiku (located at Luoyang in the Henan Province) and Maiji Shan Shiku (located at Tianshui of the Gansu Province) are known as the four biggest Shiku of China. Mogao Ku is renowned for its colourful drawings on the wall of the caves, and it is also the biggest existing art gallery in the world.

The drawings in the caves are about various Buddhist stories, which convey different positive messages about life, and are the essence of the art in the cave. These stories on the wall are always simple and they are all brilliantly drawn, educating people to be good and to believe in the Buddha. The drawings were originally drawn to provide a more beautiful background for the Buddhist statues in the caves, but now they have become outstanding pieces of the Shiku art in the world.

If Mogao Ku is a huge gallery for murals, then Maiji Shan

Mogao Ku

Shiku is a huge gallery for sculptures. At present, there are 194 caves in Maiji Shan Shiku, in which there are over 7,000 statues and sculptures made of clay and stones. Those that are made of clay are the most famous. The sculptures here are of different sizes, they could be as small as just over twenty centimetres tall and as large as fifteen metres tall; their faces have different emotions and they are all in comfortable postures. People call it "the Eastern Sculpture Gallery". Maiji Shan has a height of 142 metres, and the mountain is too steep to climb in most parts. However, with the help of only some simple hammers and ropes, it is amazing that ancient people managed to dig so many caves and make so many brilliant sculptures in them. Some of the caves are 20 to 30 metres above ground, but some others are 70 to 80 metres above ground, so this is unbelievable.

Chinese Shiku are a treasure of Buddhist art and reflect social, traditional and religious elements. Shiku art represents the development of art and humanity studies in China; however the remaining art work is now damaged by over-development of tourism and over-exposure to the public. It is said that the large amount of carbon dioxide exhaled by numerous tourists causes deterioration of the drawings. In addition, they are constantly destroyed by erosion from wind, dust and sand. This unfortunate situation is compounded by random illegal people drawing things on the wall or even smuggling the ancient treasures out of the caves.

Apart from the Shiku, the art of creating gardens is also historically famous in China. It matches well with the natural mountains and lakes, and at the same time shows a harmonious relationship between nature and people. Cultivated gardens can be divided into two types, royal gardens and private gardens. Both kinds of gardens put a lot of emphasis on the settings of natural things on earth. For example, the royal gardens in the Qing Dynasty (1644 – 1911) are huge, where the mountains, lakes and plants in them are all original, giving a luxurious and elegant outlook. Chengde Summer Resort, with 72 scenes, is the largest Qing royal garden of all. It can be divided into the lakes area, plains area and mountains area, and it contains a mixture of different kinds of gardening techniques.

Whereas for the private gardens, which are a lot smaller in terms of size, various techniques like "borrowing scenes", "piling up mountains and lakes" and "clever placing of plants" are used to create spaces. "Borrowing scenes" refers to the skill of "borrowing" the non-existent scenes to expand the actual scene. Ji Chang Garden in Wuxi uses this technique, together with the clever design of buildings. People can see the Long Guang Pagoda as if it is a part of the garden, when in fact it is outside the garden. Consequently, the size limitations are minimized.

Chinese creative gardening is famous not only for its delicate settings, but also for its ability to show the inner feelings of the designer. For example, the name of the garden is a big hint. There was a government official called Wang Xianchen, who eventually chose early retirement because he was disappointed with the large number of corrupt officials in the government. He then gave his garden in Suzhou the name Zhuo Zheng Garden, with the vocabulary "Zhuo Zheng" taken from a saying about an emperor's poor quality of rule.

Chapter 6

Language and Literature

永和九年歲在癸丑暮春

于會稽山陰之蘭亭修禊

也群賢畢至少長咸集

此地有崇山峻領茂林脩竹又有清

流激湍映帶左右引以為流觴

列坐其次雖無絲竹管絃

盛一觴一詠亦足以暢敘

幽情是日也天朗氣清惠風和

1 National Language and Local Dialects

China is a huge country. Different local dialects are used in different regions, so people from different regions may fail to communicate with each other using their own dialect. For the better growth and development of a country, there must be a common language to facilitate communication among people within the country. Mandarin (also known as Putonghua) is the national language of China. So no matter which province you come from, as long as you speak Mandarin, you can communicate with other Chinese people. At present, it is a requirement for Mandarin to be used in all formal procedures, for example, a person must know Mandarin well enough before he can be considered to be a government official, qualified to be a teacher, or work in the service sector. However, in informal situations, local dialects are still widely used, such as in family gatherings, chatting between friends, and some art performances. Therefore, local dialects cannot be replaced.

Mandarin is also called Guanhua (the official language). Actually, it has existed for a long time. Back in the Yuan Dynasty (1271 – 1368), Beijing was the political, economic and cultural centre. Officials in Beijing spoke the Northern Dialect which was based on the local dialect in Beijing. Naturally, travelling merchants had to learn it as well so that they could negotiate and conduct business with those who lived in the capital city. Moreover, when government officials were designated to work in other provinces across the country, they could only speak the Northern Dialect as they most probably could not speak the local dialects of the provinces in which they were working in. As a result, for administrative purposes, when locals were dealing with the government officials, the official language would be used, and people could not join the civil service unless they were able to speak the language.

In the Qing Dynasty (1644 – 1911), schools specifically for teaching the official language were built in the Guangdong and Fujian Provinces. As we can imagine, although they learnt the official language, they could not get rid of their accents completely. Others joked that this kind of distorted "official language" as Lanqing Guanhua. ("Lan" and "Qing" mean "blue" and "green" respectively, which imply that the official language is twisted.) But then it was far better than being unable to speak it at all.

After the last emperor of China was removed, the government named Mandarin as Guoyu (the national language) and started promoting it publicly, including putting it into the school syllabus so that people had the chance to learn it from a very young age. However there was a problem: there were 56 ethnic groups in China, now that the Mandarin, which was spoken mostly by the Han people, was named "the national language", there would be a feeling that the Han people were superior to the others. Therefore after the People's Republic of China was established in 1949, the name Guoyu was changed to Putonghua, which means a "common speech" spoken by all national groups.

After more than half a century's promotion and education, Mandarin has become more and more popular among Chinese

Learning Mandarin

people. Before 1997, when Hong Kong was a British colony, Cantonese was used by the local general public and English was used in formal documents and situations. After the handover, with the consolidation of political and economic linkage between Mainland and the Hong Kong Special Administrative Region, proficiency in Mandarin is becoming increasingly vital for local people. As China joined the World Trade Organization in 2001, the enormous consumer market of China has opened to the world and its economy has leapt forward. At the same time, large international companies have set up offices in big cities in China and sent staff to work there. Because of the needs for everyday life and work, more and more foreigners ride the wave of learning Mandarin. According to the latest figures, there are hundreds of Confucius Institutes and Confucius Classrooms all over the world and the number of students learning Chinese as a foreign language has hit a record high of 40 million in 2010.

2 | Fascinating Chinese Characters

The Oracle Bones Script from the Shang Dynasty (16th century BC – 1066 BC) are believed to be the oldest readable Chinese characters. They were accidentally discovered in the 19th century, by a famous Bronze inscription specialist Wang Yirong. One day, Wang was visiting a shop selling traditional Chinese medicine, and he saw a piece of medicine where there were inscriptions on it. With his expertise in Chinese etymology, he could tell that the inscriptions were some sort of ancient Chinese characters, so he bought them all. These bones were found at the historic location that was once the capital of the Shang Dynasty. Since the inscription was made on bones, it was named the Oracle Bones Script (also known as Jiagu Wen).

The discovery of the Shang oracle bones drew the attention of many language experts across the world. They thought that they were ancient Chinese characters. Legend had it that the Yellow Emperor, the ancestor of the Chinese people, appointed Cangjie to create Chinese characters. Cangjie, supposedly, had four eyes and had the ability to explore the mystery of the world. Realistically, it is quite impossible for one person to create all the characters, so even if there was such a person as Cangjie, it may be more accurate to say that he organized and prepared the framework for Chinese characters.

There were a few stages of evolution from the Oracle Bones Script to the characters we use today. In the earlier stages, the characters were more like imitation of real objects, so they were curlier in general. In the Zhou Dynasty (1066 BC – 771 BC), they evolved into Greater Seal Script (or Dazhuan). When they evolved into Lesser Seal Script (or Xiaozhuan), a simplified form of Greater Seal Script, the characters became tidier and of similar size. These were the characters used when the First Emperor of the Qin Dynasty (221 BC – 206 BC) decided to standardize the scripts used across the whole country.

In the Han Dynasty (206 BC – 220 AD), the Official Script (or Lishu) became popular amongst the people. The biggest change here was that the lines of the characters became straighter, so the characters were generally in a square shape rather than a circular shape. From then on, the characters were more or less stabilised. It then evolved to the Regular Script (or Kaishu), where the hint of imitations of objects was almost completely eliminated. Also, when compared with the other kinds of characters, the Regular Script is the easiest to write, so it has become the most commonly-used through to today.

The shapes of characters can be divided into four categories. The first one is the imitative drafts. Characters in this category were made according to

The evolution of Chinese characters

the objects' real appearance. The second category is the indicative symbols. Characters belonging to this category were imitative drafts with a marker or an indicator, indicating what they represent specifically. The third category is the logical aggregates. For characters from this category, the two parts forming the word reveal its meaning. The fourth is the phonetic complexes. Half of each character indicates how the word is pronounced and the other half of it reveals its meaning. This is the most popular category where about 90% of all the characters belong.

In Chinese, precious items are called Baobei. Bei means shells, in the past, shells were used just like money is used these days, so we can imagine how precious it was. For all the Chinese characters that consist of the character "shells", their meanings are always related to riches and transactions, some examples are money, bribery, greed, poverty, mortgage, buy, sell, expensive, and cheap. Another interesting note is that, all the Chinese characters that represent methods of cooking have the character "fire" in them, as fire was essential for cooking at that time.

A problem for Chinese characters is that some words are complicated and involve a lot of strokes. Gradually, people started to use simplified characters instead of the original ones. During the 1950s, two hundred million Chinese people were reckoned to be illiterate. In order to fix the problem, simplified characters were formally introduced to the people in 1958. Since then, the use of simplified characters reached all levels of the society as well as the international arena. This greatly increased the efficiency in writing; however, some of the ability to reveal meaning directly from the words was lost.

3 | The Three Great Poets – Li, Du and Su

The most famous poet in China must be Li Bai (701 – 762). He is also known as "the Poet-Immortal", as his poems are so well written that it seems impossible for a human to create them. He got this nickname from He Zhizhang, a veteran poet, who was very impressed after reading his poems. The emperor at that time, Tang Xuanzong, also admired his talent a lot. In order to let him write excellent poems, the emperor would give Li a lot of wine and he would not punish him even if he acted rudely after drinking. Once, Li was half-drunk, and at that moment, the emperor would like to watch him composing poems, so he asked Gao Lishi to bring him over. Li got up, stretched his leg and asked Gao to take off his shoes for him. Gao served the emperor for years, everyone under the emperor, even the prime minister, treated him with great respect. Li was the only one who dared to bully him.

Li Bai

Nicknamed "the Poet-Immortal", Li's poems are romantic, passionate, exaggerated, and full of imagination. Myths, dreams, people and natural scenes were all combined by him into a very rich picture. He used "thousand strains of white hair" to illustrate having to bear a lot of trouble, and "the water from heaven" to describe tides of the water from the Yellow River. From the two examples above, we can see how he used his imagination to transform ordinary matters into awesome scenes.

Another popular poet was Du Fu (712 – 770). In his poems, he expresses his concerns and feelings about the war and its impact on the lives of ordinary people. So from another point of view, Du's poems are somehow like a record of the historical events of his time. This was more evident after he entered his middle age, when he experienced very unstable circumstances. At that time, he wrote a lot of poems reflecting on people's lives, and the outlook of the society before and after the two decades of instability.

Du Fu

His truthful account of life at that time and his concern for the people made the poems all the more precious, and also won him the nickname "the Poet-Sage". A very good example was his poem about a house destroyed by the wind. In the poem, he described the fact that the wind destroyed his home and the rain soaked his bed. In such a dreadful situation, Du did not moan about what happened to him, instead, he had his thoughts on the thousands of people who were as unlucky as him. In his poem, he said that if everyone could live in a safe home, even if his own was destroyed and he was left alone freezing to death, he would still be very happy.

While Li and Du were both very prominent poets in the Tang Dynasty (618 – 907), Su Shi (1037 – 1101, also known as Su Dongpo) was an outstanding artist in the Northern Song Dynasty (960 – 1127). Su was exceptionally talented in a lot of areas like writing poems and lyrics, calligraphy, painting, playing chess and music. One of the most famous stories about him was that once, Liaoguo, a neighbouring country, sent an ambassador to visit the Chinese emperor. This man was very good at poems, and he was proud of himself, to the extent of being extremely arrogant. He wanted to challenge the scholars in the palace to show off his ability. The emperor knew that Su was an expert in this area, so he sent him to take up the challenge.

The ambassador could

Su Shi

not wait, as soon as he saw Su, he suggested a topic for the poetry contest. Su smiled and answered that writing a poem was too easy, what about reading a poem? Then, Su wrote a poem at once, in his own special style. The ambassador had no clue about the poem's meaning or the language used, and from then on, his arrogance was gone. As for the poem, Su used the characteristics of Chinese characters to disguise their meaning. For example he altered the size, taking away or replacing certain parts, and swapping or reversing the positions of some parts. He wrote a word in a taller way to represent that it was long. Since the ambassador had never seen such a style of writing, he could not understand it at all. From this, we can see how talented Su was and the emperor's decision to pick him to tackle the challenge was a correct one.

Romance of the Three Kingdoms and *All Men Are Brothers*

Everyone who knows Zhuge Liang (181 – 234) in China will say that he is a great prime minister. He was also the most popular prime minister ever, which is in part due to the famous novel *Romance of the Three Kingdoms* (also known as *Sanguo Yanyi*). About 70% of what was written in the book was true; using Zhuge as the main figure,

Romance of the Three Kingdoms

this masterpiece of the Ming Dynasty (1369 – 1644) described amazing stories about him to show how outstanding he was amongst the prominent figures in the Three Kingdoms Period (220 – 280).

An unusual introduction to Zhuge in the story hints at his importance. It was said that before taking over Jingzhou, Liu Bei (161 – 223) had no strong hold. Since Liu highly valued intelligent people, Zhuge was recommended to him on the basis that he was highly intelligent. Liu believed that Zhuge, also known as "the Hidden Dragon", would be a great help to him in unifying the whole country, so he visited him in person to show his sincerity. Twice, Liu failed to convince Zhuge to help him. However at the third attempt, he finally succeeded. After Zhuge became the prime minister, he came up with a number of military strategies to defeat enemies, like "using boats to borrow arrows", "making use of the wind to burn the opponent's chained navy ships" and "the trick of an empty city" and so on.

In the Ming novel, the author Luo Guanzhong (1310 – 1385) created different images for some 400 or so figures. The main figures always had their unique personalities; this made them livelier, like Cao Cao (155 – 220) who was evil and tricky, Liu Bei who was tolerant and generous, Guan Yu who was faithful and upright, Zhang Fei who was brave and righteous, and Zhou Yu who was sceptical yet clever. Since the story was about the Three Kingdoms various attempts to defeat others, the novel shows human beings' darker qualities. It was said that the author described everything in detail because he intended to use the story as a metaphor for the society that he was living in at that time, revealing the bad side of that world and also expressing his wish for peace.

At about the same time as *Romance of the Three Kingdoms*

was written, another novel appeared: *All Men Are Brothers* (also translated as *Water Margin*, *Outlaws of the Marsh*, or *Shuihu Zhuan*). The revolt of Song Jiang and his followers was a historical fact, which later became a popular subject for story-tellers. It was about 108 heroes and heroines, from very different background, including millionaires, murderers and fishermen, who came together as a group because of their sense of righteousness. They did not care about each others' origins and helped each other out whenever needed. The author described the actions of this group of rebels, singing praises to their noble deeds such as robbing the rich to help the poor, and also eliminating criminals. The emphasis was on their daring to rebel and battle against corrupt officials, and also on their selflessness and courage to fight against corrupted power.

The Flower Monk

The 108 "brothers" had their base on a remote mountain, and while some were forced to escape from their homes, others simply felt a calling to join the rebels in their mountain hideout. Although they came together under different situations, they shared a common objective: to protest against corrupt ruling power.

For example, one of the rebels Lu Zhishen, the "Flower Monk", was originally a lower-ranked official in the army. He was frustrated by the unfairness in society. He never bowed to his powerful opponents and his motto was "My cane clears all dangerous paths and my knife slaughters all the people who gained their status unfairly." One day, he met Lin Chong, the "Leopard Head" and they recognised each other's similar loathing of corruption. Lu and Lin's hatred of corruption and power abuse led them to directly confront evil officials, in complete disregard for their own interests and even their personal safety, sticking true to the theme of "people standing up against oppression".

5 | *Journey to the West* and *Dream of the Red Chamber*

During the Tang Dynasty (618 – 907), a widely-respected monk called Xuanzhuang (602 – 664, also known as Sanzang) went over the border to India to obtain Buddhist sutras. It took him 19 years to do so, and when he came back with 657 books, it attracted great attention from the government. After he returned, the emperor requested a meeting with him and showered him with high praises. He preached to his followers about his experience, and they recorded all the interesting things, history, geography and famous sites of those distant lands.

Journey to the West

To deify him, people added some myths and legends into his journey, and character like the Monkey King (also known as Sun Wukong) were also added. All these inspired Wu Cheng'en (1500 – 1580) to create one of the four best classic Chinese novels — *Journey to the West*.

The story is about the journey westward of Xuanzhuang and his three apostles and the way they make use of their strengths and abilities to conquer the devils and temptations they meet along the way. Why did the author include the devils? The answer can be found in his background. Wu was renowned for his writing ability since he was small, but when he was in his thirties, he was still an ordinary man, making his living by writing. This humble life prevented him from developing his talents further. Hence we note that in the story, behind all the humour, there are knowledgeable people who harm society, people who were physically strong yet have evil minds, and also kings and emperors who do not run the country well. Many people, including the author, hoped that evil would be overcome by goodness.

In *Journey to the West*, Monkey King is the cleverest and is also very good at fighting. One of the many famous stories about him describes how he kicked up a fuss at the Heavenly Palace. It was said that the Monkey King was originally the king of the monkeys at the Huaguo Mountain. One day he learnt from the immortals the techniques of transforming and leaping in somersaults, then he started to think that he was too powerful to fear anyone. In order to prevent him from rebelling, the Heavenly King granted him a great title and sent him to guard the fruit garden. The Monkey King could not resist the temptation of the tasty fruits, so he ate them one by one. Later, some fairies discovered that the fruit was gone and they were frightened. The Monkey King realised that he had broken the rule, but he pretended to be innocent and asked one of the fairies why they were picking the fruit. Then the fairy told him that the Queen Mother of the West was organising a big party for all the immortals where the fruit would be the main dish.

He was even angrier after hearing this, because he was one of the members of the Heavenly community, but he was not invited to the party. Nevertheless he attended the uninvited party and consumed most of the prepared food and drinks. Being slightly drunk, the Monkey King swallowed a pill that would significantly lengthen his life. After the Heavenly King heard about this, he was in a rage that he ordered a hundred thousand soldiers to arrest him. The Monkey King fought with all his might to defend himself, and in the fight he shook Heaven and created a huge mess.

Another novel of equal importance is *Dream of the Red Chamber* (also known as *The Story of the Stone* or *Honglou Meng*). It was written by Cao Xueqin (1716 – 1763), who was born into the family of a very rich and powerful government official. During his five inspection tours to the South, Emperor Kangxi stayed in Cao's residence for four times, which showed the close relations between his family and the royal family. Being brought up in such a family, Cao led the life of the most privileged class during his childhood.

Dream of the Red Chamber

When he grew up, however, his father was dismissed from his post, and quickly became miserable and poor. This drastic change of fate had a severe impact on his career. It was during this time that he began to write his classic novel.

Dream of the Red Chamber relates the love affair between Jia Baoyu, Lin Daiyu and Xue Baochai, and also portrays how a rich, powerful family became a poor, struggling family. The main character Jia was someone who did not follow traditional norms, yet Jia was raised in an environment which emphasized tradition and moral codes. He understood that he was the son of the family so he felt he had to do the family proud, on the other hand, he did not want to be a puppet and be controlled. He refused to take the life journey that his family had chosen for him. He persisted with his belief in love, but in the end it was ruined by the overwhelming power of conservatism.

Lin was a sensitive and sentimental girl. She shared many of Jia's views on life and society. She loved him, but this love was frowned upon and opposed by the older generation, thus bringing her endless sorrows and sufferings, and finally caused her early death. As to Xue, she upheld all the expected moral principles and won the favour of those in control of the family. She was married to Jia, but the marriage did not bring her any happiness.

The author's meticulous attention to detail is one of the reasons for the novel's popularity. It took Cao ten years to write and make necessary amendments to the story. He claimed that the story was based on his personal experience, and apart from some omissions and additions, the story was very close to what actually happened. The novel was written in beautiful colloquial Chinese based on the Beijing dialect, interspersed with dialogues and poems in classical Chinese. The plot of the novel, which consisted of hundreds of incidents in daily life was very well woven with no break in the continuous development of the story. To many readers, the novel is both historically meaningful and intrinsically interesting. People who specialise in studying the novel call their work "Red Studies"; this specialist field started shortly after it was published and continues to this day.

Chapter 7

Thought and Enlightenment

1 The Contention of a Hundred Schools of Thought

During the Spring and Autumn Period (770 BC – 476 BC), Guan Zhong (725 BC – 645 BC) and Bao Shuya (? – 644 BC) were very good friends. At that time, there were troubles internally within the State of Qi, where Jiu and Xiaobai were fighting each other for the throne. Guan was Jiu's man and Bao was Xiaobai's man. Later on, Guan had a chance to assassinate Xiaobai but it was not successful. In the end Xiaobai won, and he became the king. He intended to name Bao as the prime minister, but Bao refused and suggested that Guan would be a better choice because Guan was more talented than him in running a country. The king was very surprised, and he said, "Guan once tried to kill me, and now you let him work for me?" Bao replied, "We cannot blame him for that, after all, at that time he was serving another leader."

The king accepted Bao's advice and asked Guan to be his prime minister. Just like what Bao predicted, Guan did very well and Qi became a stronger state. Some time later, Guan was very ill, before his death, he recommended one of the officials, Xi Peng, to succeed him. When this news got out someone said to Bao, "Even though you were nice to Guan yet he does not repay you even on his death bed!" Bao laughed it off, and said that the recommendation of Xi Peng was actually a sign of his loyalty to the king, because Guan knew that Bao was not the most suitable person to be the prime minister. That night, Bao visited Guan and brought the dish Guan liked most to eat. Guan was very touched, and said, "My parents gave birth to me, but it is Bao who understands me best." This story illustrates the huge demand for talent at that time, and how the use of capable people can increase the prosperity of a country.

During the Spring and Autumn Period, the leader of the Zhou Kingdom lost his status as the sole ruler of the nation because the power of the kings in different parts of his empire was growing. The kings tried their best to attract brilliant people to work for their states in order to strengthen their forces, just as the king of Qi had hired Guan, even though he had once tried to assassinate him, on the basis that Guan had the ability to govern a state. Talented people, if appreciated by kings, would become major government officials. That was why talented people travelled everywhere to promote their ideas of good governance, and as a result, many different theories and ideologies of governance appeared at this time.

Another factor that contributed to the spread of thought and theories was public education. During this period, it was common for ordinary citizens to receive education, so knowledge did not stay within the government elite; books did not just stay locked up in the family of the officials, everyone had a chance to read them and more private schools were set up, producing lots of capable people. In a diverse environment where different kings ruled their countries using different systems, people enjoyed a high degree of freedom in thinking and making speeches, and theorists were encouraged to express their views. Under such a situation, different theories were debated, tested and looked into more deeply.

Along with the social and political changes there arose

Freedom in Thinking and Debating

important philosophers and profound philosophical theories. Schools of thought appeared one after another. Each school had its main theorist and followers. Lots of books were published to propagate their views and criticize others' fallacies. Generally at that time, there were "Nine Branches" and "Ten Schools" of thought. Of the nine branches of thought, the most important ones are Confucianism (or Rujia), Taoism (or Daojia) and Legalism (or Fajia).

The Spring and Autumn Period and the Warring States Period were the golden ages of the development of thought and ideologies in China. At that time, all kinds of theories appeared, and none of the kings restricted freedom of speech and thinking in any sort of way, so these thought and ideologies were debated and expressed freely. All the great thinkers, such as Confucius (551 BC – 479 BC, also known as Kongzi), Mencius (372 BC – 289 BC, also known as Mengzi), Laozi (600 BC – 470 BC), Zhuangzi (369 BC – 286 BC) and Han Feizi (281 BC – 233 BC), all appeared in these periods and they all contributed to the blossoming of important ideas about how to rule a country effectively.

2 | Confucius the First Private Teacher

The main theme in Confucianism, which refers to the teachings of Confucius (551 BC – 479 BC, also known as Kongzi), is "Ren". According to Confucius, Ren is about people treating each other with real emotion, sincerity and respect. People should bear the same attitude towards others, no matter how close or distant they are with the other party, or whether or not they belong to the same social class, so that there will be harmony in the society. Moreover, he believed that if one limits one's desire and controls one's selfishness and greed, then one's actions would always be respectful and polite.

In fact, this can be achieved simply by ignoring things that are against common moral values and discipline. Confucius' belief was that if a king could see his citizens' happiness as his source of happiness and their worries as his own worries, together with placing a great importance on rules and regulations, then people would remain loyal to the king and the state would grow stronger. According to him, the

Confucius

most advanced stage of Ren is not only about avoiding doing things that are morally unacceptable to preserve one's life, but also about sacrificing one's life to preserve moral values.

Confucius is also seen as one of the greatest teachers ever in Chinese history. He was the first person to set up private schools so that ordinary citizens could also receive education. This was a major breakthrough back then because before that, only children of the nobles would have the opportunity to study. There were two key aspects of education which, to him, were the most important. The first was the idea that a man should be given an opportunity to study regardless of his background. At that time, everyone could attend his private school; also, the tuition fees were really low, and what is more, the age of his students differed greatly too. One of his students was just nine years younger than him while another one was 48 years younger than him.

The other important aspect was the implementation of different teaching methods for different people. It was important because he was the first teacher to recognise the variations of levels of talent and characters among individuals, and adjusted his teaching methods accordingly, so that students could learn and improve themselves more effectively. As mentioned before, the age of his students differed greatly, so using the same method to teach certainly would not be the most effective way.

Sometimes he gave different answers to the same question from different students. One famous incident was when a student asked Confucius whether he should act on constructive suggestions from others, Confucius told him to hold on for a while and seek advice from more people before working on it. When another student asked the same question, Confucius encouraged him to go ahead and act on it directly. Why did Confucius give two completely different responses? He later explained that the first student always paraded his superiority and strove to outshine others, so he often did things in a rush and handled things impulsively; while the second student was a modest person who always had a hard time in making decisions, so he often missed out opportunities while he was pondering his options. This is a great example of how Confucius taught students in accordance to their aptitude.

In regard to learning attitudes, Confucius had his views as well. Once when visiting a temple, he asked the host there for advice on certain unfamiliar rituals. This showed that he did not mind asking others when he came across something he was not sure about, even though it might look embarrassing. There is no boundary for knowledge in this world, and since people can only learn a certain amount, everyone is bound to come across something they have not learnt before. He said that in those situations, a person must be able to admit their ignorance, and be humble enough to ask so as to learn.

It was said that Confucius had three thousand students altogether. Once he brought his students with him and visited many states, promoting his idea on how to run a state. However, none of the leaders took his advice, so he went back to his home, where he put all his efforts into education and editing books. He was the founder of Confucianism, which became the most influential school of thought for more than 2,000 years. His teaching *The Analects of Confucius* (or *Lunyu*), which was a collection of his sayings and actions, is seen as a classic by all generations after him, and many of his words are still true today.

Mencius (372 BC – 289 BC, also known as Mengzi), a master of Confucianism, believed that men were originally righteous rather than evil, and that people were generally sympathetic to each other.

Sympathy is a basic trait and Confucius said that we should try to extend our kindness as far as possible. Mencius said that we should try to put ourselves into others' shoes, so that we would not harm others with something we did not want for ourselves. Moreover, by viewing the matter from another's perspective, we can develop empathy and would resist sacrificing others for our own benefit.

3 | Talent Recruitment Systems

In ancient China, it was difficult for one to step out of one's social class, because society strictly followed an order of succession based on descent lines determined by the male line. Offspring of farmers lacked motivation to change as they felt that their fate was to follow their fathers'. This succession system was obviously imperfect.

In the Western Han Dynasty (206 BC – 23 AD), Emperor Wudi (156 BC – 87 BC) recognized this problem and he carried out a reform. He ordered the local officials to select potential candidates for government officials by judging their standards of moral conduct, and ignoring family background. In this way, citizens from modest backgrounds could escape from their original lower social class. The choice of people with high moral standards also brought about a change of climate in the government.

Yet this reform was not without flaws. Since there were not any specific selection criteria, the local officials would pick their relatives or others who bribed them, which again, only the rich could do that and benefit. During the Three Kingdoms Period (220 – 280), one of the leaders, Cao Cao (155 – 220), proposed a change. He believed that in governing a country, one's ability mattered more than moral conduct, and objective requirements could be set to test one's ability. Subsequently the Nine-rank System was established, which classified the potential candidates into nine categories in the following order: upper high, medium high, lower high, upper middle, medium middle, lower middle, upper low, medium low, and lower low. The classification was done by local administrators, while the central government would treat it as a reference when it assessed the candidates in the next step of selection.

Again there was room for improvement in this system. Even though there were objective criteria for selection of candidates, the local administrators could be tempted by bribery, or they might be related to the sons of nobles, as most government officials were from rich families at that time. Therefore, in the Sui Dynasty (581 – 618), the Imperial Examinations System was introduced to replace the Nine-rank System. All men could attend the examinations, regardless of their family background. The selection was based on how well the candidates did in their exams, and the test administrators would not have any opportunity to cheat, as the names of the candidates were hidden on the exam paper. This greatly increased the probability for hardworking scholars to be government officials.

The Imperial Examinations

The Imperial Examinations System was used until the end of the Qing Dynasty (1644 – 1911), and was standardized along the way since it was first launched. The system became perfect during the Ming Dynasty (1369 – 1644) when there were four levels of examination. The first level was an exam held in each county, where every man in the respective counties could participate. The ones with the highest scores from each county could then proceed to the second level of exam, which was held in each province. And then, the top scorers from each province would take the third level of exam, which was held in the capital city. Finally, the last level of exam would be held in the palace, where the best performers in the previous stage of examination would compete against each other. The emperor would be the test administrator, and he would pick the top three candidates, who would be awarded the titles in the order of Zhuangyuan, Bangyan and Tanhua. All the candidates who could pass through the first stage of examination would become government officials, and the further they succeeded in the exam stages, the higher the rank of official they could achieve.

China was the first country to introduce such a systematic examination system, which provided access for ordinary people to climb up the social ladder. You might argue that students from this system might not have whole-person development in their education, and having one exam only at each stage might be too harsh. You could be right, but for a country with so many people (up to 200 million in the late Ming Dynasty) and limited resources, this would no doubt be the most efficient way to recruit talent.

4 Filial Piety and Marriage

The Chinese put a lot of emphasis on virtues and manners, and filial piety, which means a respect for parents and ancestors, is held above all else. In somewhat general terms, filial piety means to be good to one's parents and take care of them. It could also refer to keeping the good conduct not just towards parents but also to the community so as to win respect for one's family. One should also perform one's job well so as to obtain the material means to support parents as well as carry out ritual to one's ancestors. People were encouraged not be rebellious; to show love, respect and support; display courtesy; ensure male heirs and uphold fraternity among brothers; wisely advise one's parents, including dissuading them from moral unrighteousness and display sorrow when they suffer sickness and death.

Filial piety is the subject of a large number of stories. One of the most famous collections of such stories is *The 24 Filial Exemplars* (also known as *Ershisi Xiao*), which contains stories that depict how children treated their parents and ancestors well in the past. One popular story was about the Wu's family in the Qing Dynasty (1644 – 1911). The family was so poor that they did not have enough money to buy food and clothing, so the parents resorted to sell their four sons to the wealthy people as slaves. The four children were very hardworking and frugal, so they managed to save enough money to buy themselves out of bondage, and by the time they had grown up. They returned to their hometown, built their homes and got married. As they loved their parents so much, they competed against each other to serve them.

Well of course, in a peaceful way. In the beginning, each son took turns to house their parents for a month, so each son would meet their parents every 3 months. After a while, they felt that the 3-month period was too long, so each son took turns to house their parents for a day instead. Subsequently, it became unbearable not seeing their parents for 3 days, so they decided to take turns to serve their parents at each meal. And every 5 days, the whole family would get together, with the sons, daughter-in-laws, and grandchildren toasting the parents endlessly. The parents lived a very happy life and greatly enjoyed their later years.

Mencius (372 BC – 289 BC, also known as Mengzi), the master of Confucianism who was mentioned earlier believed that the worst form of mistreatment of one's parents was not to produce offspring. So you could tell how important marriage was in the old days. There were a lot of rituals to observe in a traditional Chinese marriage, which were generally known as the "Three Letters" (or San Shu) and "Six Etiquettes" (or Liu Li). The marriage was initiated by a series of the Three Letters. First, the "Request Letter" was sent from the groom's family to the bride's family, formally requesting a marriage. After that, the "Gift Letter" accompanied the gifts of the groom's family to the bride's family shortly before the wedding. And finally, the "Wedding Letter" was given on the day of the wedding, officially accepting the bride into the groom's family.

The Six Etiquettes are quite interesting. The first etiquette is "Proposal", which is when an unmarried man's parents found a

Traditional Chinese Marriage

potential daughter-in-law. They would then locate a matchmaker whose job was to mediate the conflict of interests and general embarrassments when the two families discussed the possibility of marriage. The second etiquette is "Birthdates", which would take place if the potential daughter-in-law's family did not object to the proposal, and then the matchmaker would compare the couples' birthdates. According to Chinese astrology if the couple was compatible they would then proceed to the next step. The third etiquette is "Bride Price". At this point the groom's family arranged for the matchmaker to present the "Request Letter" to the bride's family.

The fourth etiquette, "Wedding Gifts" requires the groom's family to send an elaborate array of food, cakes, and religious items to the bride's family, together with the "Gift Letter". After that, the fifth etiquette is "Arranging the Wedding", where the two families would arrange a wedding day that would bring the most luck to the couple, again based on the Chinese calendar. Finally, the last etiquette is "Wedding Ceremony", where the bride and groom became a married couple. This last step consists of many elaborate parts, including the wedding procession from the bride's home to the groom's home; the ceremonies to welcome the bride and her wedding procession into the groom's home; the actual wedding ceremony where the couple would pay respect and bow to the Buddha, deceased ancestors, the bride and groom's parents and other elders, as well as to each other; and finally the wedding banquet.

Does it sound complicated to you? You might be surprised to hear that some of the above customs were passed on until today, such as sending wedding gifts to the bride's family, arranging a wedding day based on the Chinese calendar, and the wedding procession from the bride's home to the groom's home and so on. After all, marriage is a significant milestone in one's life, so most people would like to have an extravagant wedding ceremony so as to have good memories of the important occasion.

5 Taoism and the Harmony with Nature

The very first ancestor of the Chinese was the Yellow Emperor (also known as Huang Di), and he is widely regarded as the person who laid down the principles of Taoism. One day, at the end of the Spring and Autumn Period (770 BC – 476 BC), someone who was very good at astrology observed that something special occurred in the sky and predicted that a saint was about to appear. Soon after that, an old man on a funny carriage arrived. The old man was warmly greeted by the person who predicted his arrival, and was invited to write down some wise words for people in the world to learn about. The old man was Laozi (600 BC – 470 BC), who wrote up the *Tao Te Ching* (also known as *Daode Jing*). Laozi said that the basis of the universe is "Tao", which is why his thinking is called Taoism. Taoism was a philosophy originally, it advocated people to be calm always, to be rid of desire at all times, and to be as close to the natural state as possible. Later in the Eastern Han Dynasty (25 – 220), a person called Zhang Ling (34 – 156) managed to coordinate various groups which believed in Taoism. Together with the Yellow Emperor and Laozi, the three of them were known as "the Three Ancestors of Taoism".

Taoism is mainly about enhancing one's body state and inner thinking. Enhancing the body state helps one to match the cycle of nature better, so that people can live longer. There are also alchemists who produce pills for people to refill what is lost from the body as they age. In addition, the goal of enhancing inner thinking is to let people rediscover their natural character, overlook their desire and greediness, and ignore the material temptations in the world, so as to achieve contentment. Laozi believed that a person should not be too obsessed with accomplishments such that he overworks himself, and he should not worry too much about the outcome, but he should obey the rules of nature instead.

Laozi

There is a story about a person who came across a fairy, and they went for a drink together. The person complained that he was poor and his talent was not recognised by others, so he could not do something spectacular to improve the reputation of his family. After hearing it, the fairy said nothing but gave him a green pillow, and told him that sleeping on this pillow would make his dreams come true. The person did just that, and he dreamt about his future life, where he would have a nice big house, marry a beautiful wife, and become an important official in the government. His five sons were all very successful people too. However, at the end of his dream, he caught a disease where even doctors had no cure for it and he died on his bed. At this point, he was scared and he woke up. He realised that it was just a dream, and saw the fairy sitting next to him, smiling. He then realised that fame and riches were not the most important thing in life, because in the end all would become nothing, whilst it would be more important to enhance one's body state and inner thinking, so that a person might understand life completely, enjoy eternal life and not to be troubled by worries.

Zhuangzi (369 BC – 286 BC) is another representative figure of Taoism. He had a famous metaphor to explain the attitude above: a tree with poor quality wood is quite useless, but that is exactly why it is not chopped down and can last forever. Zhuangzi is famous for his unique outlook in life, and there was an interesting story about him. Once, he was walking with his friend, where they came to a pond. He told his friend that the fish in the pool was swimming happily. His friend asked him, "What makes you think that the fish is happy?" He replied, "Since you were not me, why do you assume that I do not know whether the fish is happy or not?" His friend said, "I am not you, so I cannot discern how you feel, similarly, you will not be able to understand how the fish is feeling." Zhuangzi rebutted, "When you asked me how I could tell the fish is happy, you assumed that I knew about it, that was why you posed such a question!"

From this we can see that, Zhuangzi views matter differently from ordinary people. Let us test you with a similar question. When you see a tree, what would first come to your mind? You are probably thinking, well, a tree is a living object standing on the ground, and it does not have any senses or emotions, what is so special about it? That could be right in a scientific standpoint, but if we give up this self-centred perspective, we would realise that the tree and us both exist in this world, so we actually share something in common with the tree, instead of being different from it.

Taoism, together with Confucianism and Buddhism, are the three most popular ideologies in ancient China. They also share some similar values, with all three embracing a humanist philosophy emphasizing moral behavior and human perfection. In the next section, we will talk about Buddhism.

6 Buddhism and the Truth of Life

The Chinese are a spiritual rather than a religious people. From very early times, they have been more concerned with humans and nature than gods and heaven. In order to understand the Chinese Buddhism, it is important to attain a basic knowledge of the Original Buddhism.

Shakyamuni Buddha (563 BC – 483 BC) was a human being before he became Buddha. In the name Shakyamuni, "Shakya" is a family name, while "Muni" is a title given to successful people. His original name was Siddhartha Gautama, and was born in the 6th century BC. He was an Indian prince, who was supposed to be the future king, yet in the end he became Buddha after practicing asceticism. How did it happen? The prince first saw an old person, and realized the fact that men would eventually grow old, which deeply troubled the prince. In his future outings, he came across an ill person, and then a decaying corpse, and finally an ascetic. The last person told him that living an ascetic life would help him overcome the pain of aging, illness and death. This delighted the prince, and from then on, he set his mind on leading a different life. One night, the prince left the palace, and he travelled around and witnessed many sufferings of the people. Finally, the prince became completely "awakened" when he was 35 years old, realising the true meaning of life and the root of all unhappiness —— self-indulgence and ignorance.

According to Buddhist principles, everything in this world happens in transmigration (also known as Samsara). Things are happening because something else happened in the previous life, that then produced the current situation, and the force produced by a person's actions in the current life will influence his next life on earth. This relationship is known as karma. Since there is a reason for everything, there will be consequences too. Everything in the universe is part of the phenomenon of the never-ending cycle of life and death. We should not be unrestrained or misbehave, or else we would be seeking future trouble.

Buddhists believe that the more desire a person has, the harder it will be to feel satisfied, and ultimately happiness becomes more difficult to achieve. To avoid this vicious circle, we have to reach a stage of "emptiness" where we have eliminated our desire. For example, people are trying so hard to chase after riches because the amount of riches is the measurement for success, therefore people desire for riches. If we have the concept of "riches are not eternal so they do not represent real happiness" in mind, we would not try so hard to go after them; and without such desire, we will be more likely to be satisfied and happy. When a person reaches this stage of recognizing "emptiness", then he will become an "awakened" Buddha.

There is a Chinese story about Buddhism too. Once, there was a monk called Daoyi who was living an ascetic life, enclosing himself in the room all the time. At first, his master thought he was working very hard, but later on he sensed that something might have gone wrong. The master arrived at his place and knocked on the door for a long time, yet he was not answered, so he had

Followers of Buddhism

to bang on the door very loudly to be noticed. The master said, "If you are just sitting there to give yourself inspiration, it will not work." Daoyi ignored him and went back into the house. The master then came up with an idea. He took a brick and started grinding it, making a loud noise. After a long while, he finally came out again to see what was happening, and he was surprised at the scene. The master told him that he was producing a mirror. He was even more puzzled, "It is a brick, how can you turn it into a mirror?" The master replied, "What are you doing inside? If I cannot grind a brick into a mirror, then how can you become a Buddha just by sitting in your room all the time?"

To put it simply, understanding the Buddhist principles require your heart and your mind to realize and accept, instead of merely practising the rituals. As long as you come to understand them, no matter what actions you take and where you carry them out, you would make a good Buddhist.

Chapter 8

China and the World

1 Fifty-six Ethnic Groups as a Nation

Have you ever heard about Beijing, the capital city of China? Tiananmen Square, a large plaza at the centre of Beijing, is the largest city square in the world. At the Square, there are 56 poles surrounding the national flag pole. And if you count the number of fountains in the Golden Water River (or Jinshui He) under the stone bridge, which is again, 56.

You might be wondering, why is 56 the magic number? The reason behind is that China has a total of 56 ethnic groups. Most Chinese are Han people, while the following top five ethnic groups in the order of population are Zhuang, Manchu [the rulers of the Qing Dynasty (1644 – 1911)], Hui, Miao and Uyghurs. Other prominent ethnic groups that you might be familiar with include Mongols [the rulers of the Yuan Dynasty (1271 – 1368)], Tibetans, Kazakhs, Nakhi, Bai, Hani, Li, Qiang, Yao and Yi. Different ethnic groups have different living environment, economic activities, customs and manners, as well as religions, so each ethnic group is unique. This enriches the Chinese culture.

How did so many ethnic groups come together to form China as a country? This started in the Qin Dynasty (221 BC – 206 BC). The emperor was very ambitious, he did whatever he could to invade and defeat the local leaders who resisted his rule, and eventually united the whole country. The emperor believed that his merits and achievements far surpassed the kings in previous dynasties, so he named himself the "Emperor" to show his superiority. He also wished that the Qin Dynasty could last forever, as he could pass his throne to his eldest son, who would then pass on to his eldest grandson, so on and so forth. So he named himself the "First Emperor of the Qin Dynasty" (also known as Qin Shihuang), and ordered that his eldest son to be named the "Second Emperor", and his eldest grandson be named the "Third Emperor". Unfortunately, the Qin Dynasty only lasted for two generations.

Despite the relatively short duration of the Qin Dynasty, the First Emperor made significant contributions to the cultural and economic development of China. He was responsible for a unified writing system, so all cities and all people would use one set of characters. This enabled written communication within the country and brought about exchange of culture and knowledge. In addition, the First Emperor established a new currency system to be used throughout the country, so there would not be any currency exchange problems and arbitrary issues. This facilitated the flow of trade between cities, which led to a more efficient economy. Moreover, he unified the measuring and weighting system, which helped to eliminate conflicts when people from different cities conducted businesses, as they could rely on a common standard.

Having 56 ethnic groups living together in a country, it is almost inevitable to have conflicts among themselves. They might go to war and settle the problems by force, but this would cost human lives and create a lot of damage to the society and the economy. Are there any ways for them to live peacefully together?

In the past, different ethnic groups would send representatives to build marital relations, for example, the son of the leader of

Manchu would marry the daughter of the leader of Mongols, so as to symbolize a close affiliation between Manchu and Mongols. Ethnic groups would trade among themselves, for example, the Han people living in Central China would trade tea leaves and cloths for horses and animal skins from the Tibetans. This would be mutually beneficial as each ethnic group could produce what was best and exchange these goods with others. This corresponds to the economic theory of comparative advantage.

At present, the Chinese government issues a lot of policies to encourage communication and blending of ethnic groups. One example would be its sponsorship for an annual sports event that features traditional sports originated from different ethnic groups. This section ends with a popular song that promotes the unification of ethnic groups. The lyrics go like this,

"56 stars and 56 flowers,

56 brothers and sisters are from the same family,

56 languages converge to one sentence, which is,

Love my China!"

Ethnic groups

2 China's Expansion and Its Interactions with the West

Throughout Chinese history, there are three prominent figures that are of significant importance: Confucius (551 BC – 479 BC, also known as Kongzi), the First Emperor of the Qin Dynasty (259 BC – 210 BC) and the Emperor Wudi in the Han Dynasty (156 BC – 87 BC). Confucius is regarded as the first private teacher in the nation, and he set up an excellent model of education for hundreds and thousands of generations after him. Qin's ruler the First Emperor of China, presented in the previous section, united the whole country and unified important systems such as the Chinese characters, currency, measuring and weighting metrics.

On the other hand, the Emperor Wudi is relatively less well known, but his achievements should not be underestimated. His major contribution was to expand the territory governed by China. Although it was mentioned that there are 56 ethnic groups in China, the territory under the rule of the Qin Dynasty (221 BC – 206 BC) did not include the Western and Northern regions, so when we say that Qin's First Emperor made it possible to bring together the whole country, far less than 56 ethnic groups were actually integrated at his time. It was Wudi who expanded the territory to cover the Western and Northern regions.

Wudi showed his ambition and intelligence at an early age.

When he was 9 years old, his father, the then emperor, asked him if he had the confidence to be the next ruler of the country. He replied courageously, "Yes certainly, and if there are rebellions, I will lead an army to defeat them." At that time, the Western Han Dynasty (206 BC – 23 AD) faced frequent attacks from the Huns (also known as Xiongnu) in the Northern region, yet there were not enough horses for the war, so his father asked him what he would do to fix the situation. He thought for a while and said, "We should first conquer the Western region, as they have the largest number and the best breed of horses. After that, we would have the ability to conquer the Northern region as well."

After he became the emperor, he appointed his general, Zhang Qian (? – 114 BC), to be the envoy of Han and build relationships with the Western region, with the ultimate goal of conquering the tribes in the West and the Huns in the North. Zhang took some soldiers with him and they travelled along to the Western region. On their way, they had to get close to the Northern border near the Huns, and unfortunately Zhang was captured by the Huns. The leader of Huns loved to keep Zhang at his place, as he was fascinated with the culture of the Central China region. The leader gave him a Hun wife, and ordered his soldiers to watch him closely to prevent him from escaping.

Ten years passed by, and the leader of the Huns started to pay less attention to monitoring him. Zhang took this opportunity to flee with his family and soldiers to Dayuezhi, a tribal area in the Western region. He was welcomed by the leader of the tribe, and stayed there for over a year before deciding to go back to China. On his way, he had to pass through the Hun's border, where he was recaptured. He was forced to remain there for another year or so, but eventually managed to get back to China.

Zhang's voyage to the West

Historians regarded Zhang's voyage to the Western region as "digging holes" between Central China and the Western region. The phrase symbolized Zhang's achievement to break through the imaginative wall between the two regions. His voyage paved the way for the development of the Silk Road. After his voyage, economic activities and cultural exchange between the Han Dynasty and the Western region improved by leaps and bounds. Chinese inventions and technologies such as steel making, well digging and paper making were spread to the Western region, and Chinese products such as silk, lacquer ware and bronze mirrors were further transferred from Central Asia to West Asia, and hence further to Europe. In return, Western music and dances, Persian and Greek art, Buddhism, as well as Western products including grapes, walnuts and guavas were introduced into China. Since silk was the most popular Chinese product to be exchanged, historians named this route as the "Silk Road".

As you can see, trade between China and the West has

existed for over 2,000 years. After China joined the World Trade Organization in 2001, trade volume has been increasing. With China's relatively low cost of production and high productivity of labour, China has become the largest exporter in the world.

3 Prosperity and the Spread of Buddhism

Another emperor of note is the Emperor Taizong (599 – 649). He was an outstanding politician and militarist in the Tang Dynasty (618 – 907). During the 23 years of his rule, China was at one of its most successful periods, where the economy was very strong and the society was harmonious. There was even a saying that people at that time never closed their doors at night, as there were not any thieves around and people did not have to worry about losing their valuables. How did he achieve this?

One reason is that Taizong was extremely self-disciplined. He believed that the only way to be a successful emperor was to put people's interest first. He understood that all citizens would love to have a peaceful and prosperous society. In order for him to create such an environment, he had to work day and night to find the optimal solution to solve a given problem, and establish good policies to ensure productive atmosphere. In fact, self-discipline is regarded by historians as the basic quality that emperors, or successful individuals, should possess.

You might be thinking, being self-disciplined is not that difficult, did Taizong have more exceptional qualities? He was a very good leader to work with, and he was receptive to suggestions and criticisms. He once said that "Using bronze plates as a mirror, you can wear your clothes properly; using history as a mirror, you can learn the reason for the prosperity and decline of each dynasty; using your people as a mirror, you can understand what are the things that you are doing right and wrong." He had a loyal courtier who was brave enough to express disapproval when he made mistakes. When that courtier died, he mourned about losing a precious mirror.

Taizong was also a keen believer in Buddhism. He ordered a monk, Xuanzhuang (602 – 664, also known as Sanzang), to travel to the Western region to learn about Buddhism from India and bring knowledge back to China. This reminds us of the story called *Journey to the West*, which is one of the four great Chinese novels. He became one of the main characters of the story. Even though the story was fictional and exaggerated, the major story line was based on facts. For example, he really travelled to the Western region with only one horse. He walked tens of thousands of miles, visited over 20 countries, passed through Central Asia and arrived at

Emperor Tang Taizong

India. During his journey, he encountered mirages when he went through deserts, climbed steep and windy snowy mountains, and was attacked by robbers along the way. It was a really tough expedition.

Xuanzhuang had strong will power, and he made his dream come true which would be considered "mission impossible" for most of us. After practicing Buddhism in India for 19 years, he went back to China and brought 657 books of the Buddhist sutras with him. He wrote a book, recording his experience on his journey, including the history, customs, religions, and geographical location of each country that he visited. It was a very important publication on the history of transportation and culture of China and the Western region. The book was particularly detailed on the description of India, because he had explored India thoroughly. At that time, there were 80 counties in India, and he went to 75 of them. Therefore, this book provides important information for those who study the ancient history of India.

4 Communication between China and the World

Nowadays many people love to visit China. According to some statistics distributed by the World Tourism Organization, two cities in China are frequently ranked as the top 10 most visited cities in the world, and they are Hong Kong and Shanghai. (For your information, the top 3 cities are Paris, London and Bangkok.)

In fact, foreigners were attracted to visit and live in China for a very long time, and the most famous one was the Venetian Marco Polo (1254 – 1324). There was a story behind how Marco Polo made his way to China. It was during the Yuan Dynasty (1271 – 1368), when Kublai Khan (1215 – 1894) was the emperor. One day, Marco Polo's father and uncle met a Mongolian ambassador. After chatting for a while, the ambassador noticed that they were Europeans. Since he knew that the emperor had been longing for an encounter with Europeans, he got very excited and asked if they would like to visit China with him and meet the emperor. As both of them were adventurers, they accepted the invitation eagerly. Just as expected, the emperor was extremely happy to meet them, and he asked them many questions about the customs and traditions in Europe. The emperor also requested them to pass his greetings to the Pope when they returned, and invited some missionaries to come over to China.

Marco Polo's father and uncle went back to Europe soon afterwards, and Marco grew deeply interested in their experience and became fascinated about China. He begged them to take him on their next trip to China. The three of them went to China again after a few years, carrying the Pope's letter. The emperor was very glad, and they won his trust and respect. Since Marco Polo was smart and modest, and he could speak many languages, the

Marco Polo

emperor liked him the most. He was appointed to be a government official, and he even represented China to visit other countries. He stayed in China with his father and uncle for as long as 17 years.

After he returned home, he noted down all his interesting occurrences in China, and wrote the book *The Travels of Marco Polo* (an authoritative version does not exist, the most popular English translation was published in 1938, based on the Latin manuscript which was found in 1932), and is popular worldwide until today. This is the earliest reading that introduced China to Europeans in a relatively systematic way. In the 14th to 15th centuries, European geologists drew the preliminary version of the world map based on the description of the location of Asia and China in this book. The book not only recorded his travels, but also included contents on China's history and geography, as well as its contemporary technology, such as astronomy and the calendar system, construction of bridges, production of paper, making of salt, and the use of coal. His book helped to introduce China to the Europeans, which was considered to be a mysterious country at that time. He made significant contribution to the exchange of culture between the East and the West, and the future development of a closer relationship between these two regions.

Not only do foreigners like to visit China, Chinese people also travelled overseas as well. The most famous Chinese traveller is Zheng He (1371 – 1433), a eunuch in the Ming Dynasty (1369 – 1644). He went on a series of 7 naval expeditions to the Western Ocean with a huge fleet. On his last voyage, his fleet consisted of over 27,000 people, including sailors, secretaries, doctors and translators. For each expedition, there would be 60 to 100 ships, in which the largest one was as long as 138 metres and as wide as 56 metres. It could carry over 1,000 people and a large amount of equipment. These ships were the most technologically advanced at that time, equipped with compasses and maps. He went to more than 30 countries in these expeditions, he travelled as far south as Indonesia, as far north as the Persian Gulf and Mecca, and as far west as Somalia in Africa. So he discovered Africa earlier than the Europeans by over 50 years.

Zheng's journey had a peaceful mission, his goal was to show other countries the strength of China, and his large army awed most would-be enemies into submission. These tours improved the cultural exchange and economic activities between China and foreign countries, and enhanced communication between them. In each expedition, he brought Chinese goods such as silk, tea leaves, lacquer ware and porcelain to exchange for precious products from other countries, for example, gemstones, pearls, corals and spices. On his return to China after each voyage, many countries would send envoys to visit China and present their gifts. This helped to cultivate relationships between China and other countries around the world.

5 The Four Great Inventions

So far, we have focussed on the arts and literary works. However, to be regarded as one of the four ancient civilizations (the other three are Babylon, ancient India, and ancient Egypt), China has more to offer. Chinese people are proud that their ancestors produced the "Four Great Inventions" —paper, printing, the compass, and gunpowder.

Paper was invented by Cai Lun (50 – 121), a eunuch in the Eastern Han Dynasty (25 – 220). At that time, people wrote on either bamboo slips or silk. However, bamboo slips were too heavy and were not convenient to carry, while silk was too expensive and unaffordable by ordinary people. Cai aspired to revolutionize the raw materials and technology of paper making. He believed that hemp fibre and tree skin was suitable and these ingredients were easy to obtain, so he decided to use them as the raw materials. He soaked them in water until they became a thick liquid, and then spread the mixture thinly on bamboo sheets. After drying, the liquid spread condensed and became paper. This kind of paper was white and delicate, and was very suitable for writing. The technology of paper making became very popular in China, and it was passed on to Vietnam, Korea, Japan, Arabia, and further to Europe. The invention of paper making was an important catalyst for the spread of culture and written communication.

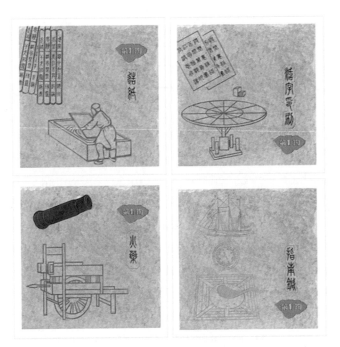

The Four Great Inventions

Printing was another significant invention in China. In the old days, people had to make copies manually by hand. The ancient Chinese resolved the problem by inventing woodblock printing. The way to do it was first to write the words to be copied on a piece of translucent paper, and then flip the paper, and stick it on a piece of wood. After that, a craftsman would carve out the wood around the reversed words. A woodblock was then created, and it could be used to make as many copies as you want, as long as you had enough ink.

Now what if an author makes some slight changes in his book and would like to publish an edited version? All the woodblocks could not be reused. And in fact, there are many words that are commonly used in all topics, so carving them each time would be a waste of effort. Moreover, having to use so many woodblocks is a waste of resources. Therefore in the Northern Song Dynasty (960 –

1127), a person called Bi Sheng (990 – 1051) invented a movable type. The idea was to craft each word on small pieces of clay, and plug them onto metal plates in the right order when printing. The small clay blocks were removable and reusable, so it became very convenient for publication.

The next major invention that we would like to introduce is the compass. It was said that the Yellow Emperor invented the first compass, which was called the "Car Guide" or "Sinan Car". On the Car Guide, there was a wooden person, whose hand would point to the south direction no matter which direction the car was moving towards. The compass was gradually improved to a version that we are more familiar with today, and starting from the Song Dynasty (960 – 1279), boats were installed with compasses, so major progress was made in sea expeditions as a result.

Gunpowder is another key invention worth mentioning. In the past, there were Taoist monks who focused mainly on the purification of one's spirit and body in the hopes of gaining immortality through the practice of Qigong, and the consumption of various concoctions known as alchemical medicines. In the Eastern Han Dynasty (25 – 220), a Taoist monk invented gunpowder accidentally when he was producing alchemical medicines! The technology advanced slowly and had begun to be used in military since the Song Dynasty. In the late 13th century, Europeans came to understand China's knowledge in gunpowder from some Arabic books, and this then became a milestone for the future development of European's military forces.

6 Other Scientific and Medical Breakthroughs

The "Four Great Inventions" were the main technological breakthroughs achieved by the Chinese, yet there are some other inventions and advancements worth noting. In the scientific arena, a scientist in the Eastern Han Dynasty (25 – 220) called Zhang Heng (78 – 139) invented the first seismograph. The device was not only practical, but it was quite artistic as well. It was a large bronze vessel, about 2 meters in diameter; at eight points around the top there were dragons' heads holding bronze balls. When there was an earthquake, one of the mouths would open and drop its ball into a bronze toad at the base, making a sound and supposedly showing the direction of the earthquake. This invention detects earthquakes, and it is one step forward for the invention of a device that anticipates earthquakes, which would be extremely helpful to prevent the loss of human lives.

Another famous scientist is Shen Kuo (1031 – 1095), a polymath scientist in the Northern Song Dynasty (960 – 1127) who published a popular book entitled *Mengxi Sketches and Notes* (also known as *Mengxi Bitan*). It was an extensive book that covered topics such as astronomy, mathematics, geography, geology, physics, biology, medicine, pharmacy, and even military science, literature, history, archeology and music. The book has been greatly

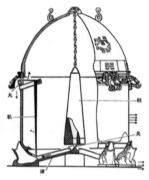

The First Seismograph

appreciated by scientists around the world through to the present, and is regarded as a milestone in the development of science in China.

In the mathematics arena, there was a magnificent mathematician named Zu Chongzhi (429 – 500) in the Southern and Northern Dynasties (420 – 589). He was the first person in the world to derive π to a very accurate extent that covered 7 decimal places. (For your information, π is a mathematical constant whose value is the ratio of any circle's circumference relative to its diameter.) It was over a thousand years later when German and Dutch mathematicians derived the same results. His contribution to mathematical society was undeniable, so it is publicly recognized that π is also called the Zu's Constant.

In addition to the achievements in science and mathematics, ancient Chinese were also leading in the medical and pharmaceutical arena. A prominent figure is Hua Tuo (145 – 208), a doctor in the Eastern Han Dynasty (25 – 220). He was known to be an excellent surgeon, and the most famous incident was performing surgery on Guan Yu (? – 208), one of the three brothers from the brotherhood of Liu-Guan-Zhang that we presented in Chapter 1. Guan was shot by a poisoned arrow in a battle, and Hua was called to help. He examined the wound carefully, and discovered that the poison had reached his arm bone, and it had to be cured immediately otherwise he might lose his arm. Since there weren't any anesthetics at that time, Hua performed the surgery while Guan was fully conscious. The surgery was a success, but how many people could be as courageous as Guan in withstanding the pain? Later, he invented anesthetics and solved this problem. This invention preceded a Western equivalent by over 1,000 years.

Another person we should know about is Li Shizhen (1518 – 1593) from the Ming Dynasty (1369 – 1644). Li was a doctor, but he was better known for being a pharmacist. He used 27 years to publish the book *Compendium of Meteria Medica* (also known as *Bencao Gangmu*, first draft completed in 1578), which consisted of 52 chapters and over 1.9 million words. The book recorded 1,892 kinds of Chinese herbal medicine, including sources from animals, plants and minerals, and there were 1,160 pictures for illustration, as well as 11,096 formulas to cure various diseases. Copies of the book were brought to Japan, Korea, Vietnam, and even Europe, and it had been translated into many languages such as Japanese, French, German, English, Russian and Latin. The book had more than 60 versions, and it became an important reference point in medical research. People worldwide recognized this book as a "Masterpiece in medicine from the East". Charles Darwin, the founder of the theory of evolution, paid tribute to Li's publication as the "Encyclopedia of China".

Apart from these famous doctors and the use of herbal medicine, there is one aspect that catches worldwide attention as well, which is the Chinese medical practice of pulse taking and acupuncture. Some people may still find these practices mysterious, yet they are scientific and have proved to be effective. Pulse taking can detect one's illness. The pulse on the left wrist demonstrates the conditions of one's heart, liver and kidneys, while that on the right wrist demonstrates the conditions of the lungs and spleen. Doctors can discover the root cause of one's disease by taking one's pulse. Acupuncture can improve one's immune system, so the patient can recover naturally, while it also relieves symptoms and pain. It is most effective in curing sciatica and backache.

7 | New Culture Movement

When the last dynasty, Qing Dynasty (1644 – 1911) collapsed in 1911, and the last emperor fled the political scene, the Republic of China was founded in 1912. By then, Western culture was widely spread among the Chinese scholars. They had a classical education but began to revolt against Confucian culture. They called for the creation of a new Chinese culture based on global and Western standards, especially democracy and science.

One of the founders of the New Culture Movement was Chen Duxiu (1879 – 1942). He also founded the journal *New Youth* (also known as *Xin Qingnian*) in 1915, which became the most prominent of hundreds of new publications for the new middle class. He introduced Mr. De and Mr. Sai to his readers, and the following is an excerpt of the dialogue between the two of them.

De: Hi everyone! My name is Democracy. I am from the West.

Sai: Hello! My name is Science.

De & Sai: We are coming to China, because we would like to promote the belief of democracy and freedom, as well as to encourage youngsters to go after the spirit of scientific research.

In case you are not aware of, the pronunciation of "De" and "Sai" in Mandarin were the first syllables of "democracy" and "science" in English. Look at how innovative Chen was in his attempt to arouse public interest!

The New Culture Movement aimed to improve the status of China, which was rather autocratic and superstitious in political thinking. Cai Yuanpei (1868 – 1940), one of the founders of the Movement was educated in Europe, and became the President of Peking University. He pushed for reforms aggressively, embraced the idea of educating boys and girls together in the same school, and proposed a new style of education that abolished

New Youth

the rote learning of the Chinese classics. He was also critical of traditional customs and practices of Chinese culture, and he was an advocate of feminism.

Cai had once published a "personal" advertisement to seek a bride, the qualities and conditions are listed as follows:

1. The woman should not have her feet bound. (Foot binding was almost mandatory back then, which first developed as a symbol of upper-class status as girls would not be able to do household chores with their disabled feet. Later bound feet were considered erotic and attractive to men.)

2. The woman must be literate. (Girls were not allowed to attend schools in the old days. They were forced to learn embroidery and weaving instead.)

3. He promised not to have more than one wife. (It was very common for men to have several wives and concubines. They were proud of having big families since this was a show of status. Some emperors were even known to have 3,000 concubines.)

4. The woman could remarry after his death. (Traditionally women who remarried would bring disrepute to herself and her family. On the other hand, widows were praised for their faithfulness.)

5. The woman could divorce him if she could not get along with him. (Divorce initiated by women was almost never heard of in the old days. Again, it would be detrimental to the reputation of the women and her family.)

The New Culture Movement brought in a lot of new elements into the development of Chinese intellectual thoughts, culture and ideology. A popular idiom goes, "Failing to advance is to go backwards", the Chinese believe that in order to be a future leader in a fast-changing world, they not only had to keep the good parts of their traditional values, but they also have to learn from other civilizations to keep up with the times.

Appendix

A Brief Chronology of Chinese History

Xia Dynasty	21st century BC – 16th century BC
Shang Dynasty	16th century BC – 1066 BC
Western Zhou Dynasty	1066 BC – 771 BC
Spring and Autumn Period	770 BC – 476 BC
Warring States Period	475 BC – 221 BC
Qin Dynasty	221 BC – 206 BC
Western Han Dynasty	206 BC – 23 AD
Eastern Han Dynasty	25 – 220
Three Kingdoms Period	220 – 280
Western Jin Dynasty	265 – 316
Eastern Jin Dynasty	317 – 420
Southern and Northern Dynasties	420 – 589

Sui Dynasty	581 – 618
Tang Dynasty	618 – 907
Five Dynasty	907 – 960
Liao Dynasty	907 – 1125
Northern Song Dynasty	960 – 1127
Southern Song Dynasty	1127 – 1279
Western Xia Dynasty	1038 – 1227
Jin Dynasty	1115 – 1234
Yuan Dynasty	1271 – 1368
Ming Dynasty	1369 – 1644
Qing Dynasty	1644 – 1911